Praise for Self Empowerment

"I was very impressed. An accurate portrayal of what's happening in the world today [with] new and powerful concepts."

JIM KEYSOR
Chairman, Keysor-Century Corporation

"A must-read for a healthy life and to be prepared for the immediate future."

HYLER BRACEY, Ph.D.
President and CEO, The Atlanta Consulting Group
Author, *Managing from the Heart*

"Finally, after managing thousands of people, this book taught me the best management principle of all: Manager, Manage Thyself — from the heart. If you manage anything from household to large corporation, manage to read this book and pass it on — It Works!"

DELMUS WALKER
President, Capitol Funding

"At last the secret truth of Self Empowerment is acknowledged clearly and simply so that anyone can live it. This system is a breakthrough in stress reduction; in business effectiveness; in bringing quality to relationships; and in simple, clear, effective living!"

DAVID MCARTHUR
Minister, Unity Church of Spokane

"A most timely product for an age of expanding democratic rights. 'Power to the people,' in the most meaningful sense, demands an empowerment of the individual, something to which this book is dedicated. Childre relates 'self-government' to effective self-management and internal balance, and outer peace to the inner peace which accompanies such balance. The book's strength is in its non-elitist approach, the author's ability to connect with the intuitive understanding of the reader, and his identification with the inner authority (our heart consciousness) rather than the outer authorities."

STEPHEN L. ROZMAN, Ph.D.
Professor & Chairman, Department of Political Science
Tougaloo College

"The most direct and to the point book on stress management that I have read. With remarkable clarity, Childre identifies our most problematic areas, shows their underlying causes and offers powerfully creative solutions. Chapter 3 alone ranks this among the most useful and insightful books in the field."

KEN CAREY
Author, *The Starseed Transmissions,*
Starseed, The Third Millenium

"Doc's idea is simple: function from the heart. Maybe we've heard that before. But this time the message appears in the vernacular: it's presented in a 'streetsense' manner that sounds do-able. Releasing stress and efficiently directing energy to ever more productive and satisfying ends are some of the benefits of heart-based choices. Female/male relationships can move toward a true partnership paradigm. Child/parent relationships can be mutually nourishing and instructive. Heart intelligence can help us find family and can expand our notion of 'family' so that all interaction is supportive. In the final analysis, heart smarts may be the only intelligence that matters."

JOYCE CHUMBLEY, Ph.D.
Educational Consultant

"Thank you. I welcome Doc's new book as a way to enhance the 'inside out' learning process."

BRADLEY WINCH, Ph.D., J.D.
Member of the Board of Directors,
National Council for Self-Esteem

"A must for anyone who seeks a happier and more balanced life. A pleasure to read."

ROBERT SCHWARTZ
President, Laurie Records

"I found the people at the Institute of HeartMath to be virtually stress-free, open and generous, highly talented and clearly focused. Their message of 'coming from the heart' is evidently not only a message but also their lifestyle."

JIM CATHCART
Author, *Relationship Selling*
Motivational speaker

A Planetary Publications Release

IN COOPERATION WITH

THE INSTITUTE OF HEARTMATH

Self Empowerment

The Heart Approach to Stress Management

Common Sense Strategies

DOC LEW CHILDRE

Planetary Publications

SELF EMPOWERMENT

THE HEART APPROACH TO STRESS MANAGEMENT: COMMON SENSE
STRATEGIES

Copyright © 1992 Planetary Publications

PUBLISHED BY

Planetary Publications

P.O. Box 66 • Boulder Creek • California • 95006 • USA

800-372-3100 • 408-338-2161 • Fax 408-338-9861

Library of Congress Cataloging-in-Publication Data

Childre, Lew, Doc, 1945-

Self empowerment : the heart approach to stress management;

common sense strategies / by Doc Lew Childre.

p.   cm.

"Based on the HeartMath system."

1. Stress management.   2. Interpersonal relations.

3. Self-actualization (Psychology)   I. Title.

RA785.C45   1992

155.9'042--dc20   91-38576

                                                            CIP

ISBN 1-879052-16-4

Cover design and artwork by Sandy Royall
Color separations by ColorPrep, Inc.
Printed by Braun-Brumfield

Printed in the United States of America

10 9 8 7 6 5 4 3 2 1

Table of Contents

Author's Foreword
My First Appreciation of Self-Management

As a child I was unmanageable. Hating self-responsibility came as natural to me as eating. Little did I know then, that I would write a book on self-empowerment through personal energy management. I guess I'm proof that it's never too late to change.

My family attempted to teach me responsibility, but my stubbornness overruled the process. Though not a Catholic, I was placed in a Catholic school at an early age. This is because it had a reputation for teaching management and respect along with education. Because of my hard-headed behavioral patterns, the first six months of Catholic school seemed like a reformatory. My conduct did eventually improve but I don't know if it was because of my perseverance or that of the teachers. Through my seven years there, I never made good grades, but I never did anywhere else either. Do you think it was me or the school systems? Of course it was me all along.

After the Catholic school tamed me, I was still unprepared for the culture shock which was ahead of me. That's when I left the Catholic school to go to a public high school. The difference between the two systems quickly made me appreciate where I had been—especially the self-management aspect. The conduct, management and respect level of the students in the new school was of another world. Respect wasn't even a word in that high school's dictionary. You only witnessed management when the students fell asleep at their desks, exhausted from rampages. It was so wild that it would have made even the Catholic nuns shrink into penguins and head for Antarctica! Humor, of course. I love and respect those sisters (nuns) more than ever, now that I can appreciate that self-management and respect for others is more important than the touted educational degrees. Anyway, I adapted and made it through public school.

I tell this story only to share with you my first awareness of the efficiency of self-management. I didn't like management but I found myself learning to appreciate it. After high school, I enlisted in the National Guard and was sent to California for basic training. It was time for me to experience another level of discipline and management. Keep this to yourself—I cried the first night and really didn't think that I could make it through the next day. One of the toughest challenges was to clean the bathroom floors each week with a tooth brush, especially when one tooth brush was all I had to last me through basic training.

If you've been through this training, then you know the story. If you haven't, you've heard enough army stories to know it can be a humbling experience. In short, I hated it when I first arrived, yet I cried again the day that I left. I missed my buddies and had learned to love the self-responsibility. You can learn it there in a way that you can't learn it in many other places. Some of it was crude but so was I. Am I now? Humbly speaking, I choose to remain a tad that way.

So, first there was the Catholic school, then the National Guard—the first two systems to penetrate my thickness. But I still had much to learn about self-management and self-centeredness. The next teaching of life came from two marriages at an early age that I wasn't mature enough to be involved in. Lacking maturity was only the tip of the iceberg. The real problem was that I was "green behind the ears" when it came to understanding and respecting the female nature. I was the male-dominant type and didn't know the word "sensitivity" existed. I learned a lot from my experiences with women and this book will share with you my new perspectives on male and female issues.

So, after these marriages twenty years ago, I decided to find a system of self-management and peace that maintained the fun aspect. I committed myself to that. I looked into various religions, from fundamentalism to the new age, but still there was something missing for me. I intuitively felt that I had to find it within myself. Many of the teachings I read said that fulfillment is within your own heart. That strongly resonated within me, so I set out to see if it was true or to prove that it wasn't.

In the beginning I had to go through much confusion to learn what the heart voice was, yet I readily could hear self-centered thoughts pouring through my head. I knew that I definitely had a *mind* of a sort and I eventually figured out what the *heart* was. Finding the heart was just a matter of knowing how to sincerely listen. I made efforts to simplify the process of understanding the difference between the head and the heart in hopes that it would make it easier for others. This book is a result of those efforts.

With practice, it became obvious that following the heart leads to self-empowerment through learning how to manage the mind and emotions. The mind and emotions are not bad guys. However, they are spunky and work more efficiently when synchronized in a joint venture with the heart. Self-empowerment is the management and balance of the mental, emotional and physical energies within your system. This adds to the refinement of what people call the spiritual nature.

Heart management is not about anything that you don't already know inside. It's just a way to help you remember the things that are important—which people tend to forget in the midst of day-to-day stress. This system is designed to dissipate stress on contact rather than allowing it to accumulate. And it works if you work with it. It doesn't take long to see results, especially if you are making sincere efforts.

Over the past several years, more than forty people, working here at the Institute of HeartMath, have proven out this system of self-empowerment before offering it to others. We've learned to be responsible for our own energy management, resulting in efficiency, harmony in human relationships and, especially, a lot of fun. We recently released a book called *Heart Smarts: Teenage Guide for the Puzzle of Life,* which is one of our first efforts to share the effectiveness of this process of self-empowerment. We addressed teenagers first, because they are the hope for a more stress-free awareness in the future.

The following chapters are about how adults can become self-empowered through connecting with their own self-smarts. If you get only one thing out of this book that helps you eliminate stress in your life, then it was worth my effort. Read from the heart and enjoy.

Doc Lew Childre, *Institute of HeartMath*

Stress:
The Planetary
Governor

Face it, stress has become a standard household commodity—
near mandatory to say the least. However, not all people experience the same amount of stress. Some have a natural knack for
deflecting the obvious day-to-day stress factors that most people
experience. Still, there are deeper levels of stress management
that can be achieved by anyone.

In watching yourself closely, you can usually find energy
leaks in your mental or emotional nature that add much stress to
your system. Some people are positive thinking types (which is
healthy), but they still experience subtle energy drains. With a
little sincere effort, anyone can bring their personal energy leaks
progressively under management.

So, if you want a way to de-stress your life, then *self-empowerment* is a practical method. Efficient prescriptions for stress relief
are within each person. By practicing self-empowerment, you can
bring them into realization and application.

We'll discuss simple techniques to practice in the following chapters. They can produce quick results—if you are sincere in your quest for stress management. Within a few years, intelligent approaches to stress management will be at the top of the "Gotta have it" list for our increasingly frustrated society.

External situations (such as traffic jams, job anxieties, problems at home, etc.) create inner stress. When you experience stress, then hormones and other bio-chemical reactions are released in your system which can cause dis-ease and debilitation in your mental, emotional and physical nature. Learning how to manage stress develops the ability to self-regulate your hormonal patterns—meaning that you become an efficient "self-pharmacist" in a sense. Your most productive drugs are within your own endocrine system. In other words, you could stay younger longer—feel more alive and especially have more energy and vitality—depending on your hormonal flow. You influence this flow more than you may think by the management or non-management of attitudes and thought patterns. Self-empowerment gives you more capacity to generate efficient hormonal prescriptions that prevent and relieve stress patterns. This translates into health and quality living.

The system of HeartMath™ has been designed to facilitate the self-empowerment process. HeartMath involves learning how to recognize and follow the *efficient* directives of your heart intuition to become your true self. The inability to be your true self is often what prevents you from experiencing happiness and fulfillment. If children could learn that at an early age, then as adults they wouldn't have to unlearn so much in order to re-discover who they are.

HeartMath is an organized arrangement of what you may already know inside but perhaps haven't yet been able to manifest with continuity. We sincerely know from our experience at the Institute of HeartMath that this system can increase your quality and appreciation of life as it has ours.

A Global Stress Overview

Most stress that people process is *unnecessary*, yet basic human intelligence knows it not. At the present level of global consciousness, people tend to think that living with stress is natural. Well, it's not natural. It's just a result of social ignorance, but innocently so until society is educated otherwise.

Some wait and hope for *things to get better,* but it's people who have to better themselves by learning to manage their energy expenditures. It's the lack of self-government in the mental, emotional and physical aspects of your nature that leaves you vulnerable to stress overloads. By re-remembering and contacting your true self, you can alleviate personal stress—and keep it from returning.

Increasingly, the evening world news serves as a global stress report. At a sweeping glance, you realize that: foreign relations, ecology, education, politics, religion, economics, etc., are all caught in tremendous stress feedback loops. This is because of the lack of self-management within the individuals in these systems. Our social problems are not necessarily the fault of our leaders. Even if we changed leaders overnight, after the dust settled the new ones would become the next targets of blame for our collective stress. Our leaders are only mirrors of the confused mess that society as a whole has generated. The responsibility for stress and inefficiency lies within all the individuals who make up a country, state, city, community or family. It's always easier to blame problems on others, but humanity will soon realize that stress reduction and energy management start with the individual self—you.

People use stimulation as a quick fix for stress, but that's like buying candy to help an overweight problem. It's hard to bail out of the stress feedback loop when you constantly repeat the same non-efficient patterns of living and thinking.

Don't confuse stress with *creative resistance energy*. Stress dilutes your energy, while creative resistance energy can be a healthy challenge with the right attitude. For example, when you transform resistances into fun creative achievements—such as weightlifting, jogging that extra mile, meeting a deadline, closing a sale, etc.—you're still releasing positive hormones into your system. As you meet resistances, it's your attitude that regulates the amount of stress in the outcome. The balancing and management of attitudes is a key factor in understanding and dissipating stress.

You can accelerate stress relief within your own system by *learning how to follow your heart's directives* or what people call "the inner voice," "intuition," "inner knowingness," etc. This book is about how to do that. *Discovering how to follow your heart's directives is a practical key to self-empowerment.*

Many people are *living to survive* rather than to increase their quality and enjoyment of life. Survival living is definitely minus the fun and fulfillment you can have if you practice a system of self-empowerment. If you wait for the economy to balance or the wars to stop before you have peace, you could have a long wait. Or, if you wait for relationships to change, or for children to meet your idealistic expectancies, or for harmony in your workplace before you have inner peace, you may never find it.

The point I'm making is this: because of *innocent ignorance* most people's peace and security are dependent upon other people, places or things. Self-empowerment is about building your own security from within. Based on the planetary stress accumulation, it's an appropriate time for people to connect with their inner truth and realize they are well equipped to de-stress much of their internal and external environment. This can be done by training yourself to listen to the intelligent truth in your own heart.

Inside themselves, people catch glimpses of the potential of self-empowerment. Still, it's hard for them to get started in the effort to harmonize their energy patterns and attitudes. They often feel they are waiting for the spirit to move them. You may not realize that the spirit is waiting for you to hear and acknowledge the potentials it has to offer if you live from your true self—from your heart. Your inner heart feelings signal you when it's time to make attitude adjustments, but the mind often drowns out the signal. With practice you can increase your ability to hear and follow that inner voice, resulting in efficient living.

Self-Management

The power to think yourself into misery is within you and the power to *stop it* is within you also. If you've glimpsed that self-truth, then it's time to take it to the next level by acting on what you know inside. That would be a wise investment of your time in this next decade.

Many have used religion, self-help, science, new age, and other processes to facilitate personal change, peace and fun in life. I realize that individuals have been helped by these programs and will continue to be. But, the collective "HELP" systems haven't been much of a bail-out for stress problems on a global level, as of yet. For some, adherence to a system becomes a crutch or mind-set. (A mind-set is a *narrow perspective*, bound in cement, that "knows-what-it-knows" and refuses the evidenced truth of a wider perspective.)

Something is missing that is seriously needed if we are looking for basic peace, much less total peace. The missing formula is *within your own heart*. That's where you can find the primary gateway to quality living. The doctrines and by-laws of inner truth are within you. As you unfold your inner truth, you are more able to be yourself and no longer have to play plastic roles to suit others' expectations. Developing a closer relationship with your heart intuition efficiently guides you through your own energy-management process. Then you can add more quality to any system you may participate in—self-help or religion, etc.

The increasing stress condition on the planet will awaken us to the realization that we have to clean up our own mess *individually*. People will soon begin a more serious search for efficient ways to get the *stressors* off their backs. As you establish balance and harmony between your head and your heart, you gain a more intelligent perspective of what creates your stress. By applying intelligence to stress, you decrease its power to drain your energy.

The "wars on drugs" or the "wars on crime" won't be very effective until we have declared "war on stress" through individual self-management. If we even have to use references to "wars" (which we've had enough of), let's at least aim that energy towards dissipating stress-creating agents—poor attitudes, mindsets, judgments, lack of care, etc. When individuals overcome the battles within themselves—by balancing the head and heart relationship—the rest of the wars will diminish in time.

Stress reigns as a major influence over the planet thus far, though you would think that the people are in charge. They are not as of yet. There was a time when you could get lost in "your own little thing" and escape having to deal with national and international stress levels. Now, global stress is accumulating into *a force to be reckoned with* which daily affects us all. As large-scale stress increases on the planet, it will especially be experienced on the individual level—even if you are far removed from the wars or the social distortions. Other than learning management of your attitudes and contacting your own strength within, there's no lasting way of escaping the societal effects of exponentially increasing stress. Everyone is subconsciously connected to the stress of the whole planet more than they think, even if their mind is not focused on this awareness.

Articles from PEOPLE MAGAZINE, TIME and many other publications prove that it doesn't matter whether you are wealthy or poor—no one is exempt from the stress monster. Stress operates as if it had intelligence—making sure that people experience repeated energy drains daily. Realize that stress maintains its powerful momentum by living off the innocence of human ignorance. People increase their stress deficit by mechanically re-creating the same problem patterns in a merry-go-round fashion.

Recent scientific studies indicate that anger, unmanaged emotions and negative reactions to stress may increase the risk of heart disease or cancer *even more* than eating high cholesterol foods or smoking cigarettes. If you are going to diminish your stress intake, you would wisely and soberly invest in the *self-management* of your mental and emotional natures. Learning to listen to your *heart directives* is "user-friendly" and effective. You don't even have to buy anything to help you get started.

The true mentor is within each person, yet it often takes a tough dose of life before people realize this—if they ever do. Following your heart is an efficient way to merge with the mentor within and balance the energies that dictate your perceptions of life. There are a lot of philosophical formulas, yet things usually have to be broken down into plain old *streetsense* (user-friendly common sense) before they have a useful and lasting effect.

If a system of self-empowerment couldn't be converted into streetsense, then it wouldn't be valuable to humanity. Systems outside yourself can help, but it's the truth within your heart that nourishes you into self-security and happiness.

Individuals can change the "ruled-by-stress" format with a little self-initiated effort to help themselves. This book addresses the obvious stress entrapments and offers a bottom line solution which is people-friendly and feasible. Stress diminishes in the light of intelligence, so let's move on and discuss *heart intelligence* and its potentials. In starting, it's important to get a feeling for the difference between your head and your heart. The next chapter will give you a better understanding of how to do that.

The Head
and the Heart

It has been said that the longest distance that a man or woman ever travels is the distance between their **head** and their **heart**. From my perspective that is true—once you understand the meaning of it.

How would you like to "live" life rather than just live through life? Would you like to get rid of insecurities, eliminate hassles and manage your day-to-day stress? Well, it's possible. You *can do it,* and you'll surprise yourself in the process. It starts with understanding what your own heart truth is all about.

When you understand the difference between your head and your heart, you're past the halfway point in the development of a system for self-stress relief and fulfillment. In learning that difference, a simple analogy is helpful.

I know this one's mundane and often over-used, but let's slice it a different way and take a deeper look: In the past when I found myself in a gridlock traffic jam, especially while already late for an appointment, there would be a tendency to blow the horn, scream out the window, or quietly rage in silent despair.

However, on some days I faced traffic jams with a serene attitude, realizing that *life* has its jams so why not manage my energy and save myself from extra stress and depletion. When I used this approach, I noticed that I didn't feel as drained and debilitated throughout the day.

In closely studying myself, I realized that even though I was one and the same person, I was faced with *two* ways I could respond each time I found myself sitting in those traffic jams: 1) React and get into anxiety; yell at the person trying to squeeze in ahead of me, etc., or 2) Calm down and get centered, adapt, and make peace with the situation.

After observing and becoming more aware of my internal feeling patterns, I realized that when I over-reacted, leading to emotional distortion—that's when my energies were *focused in my head*. I also realized that when I faced the traffic jam with inner calmness and applied mental and emotional management—that's when my energies were *focused in my heart*. I felt as if I was finally applying common sense and experienced very little stress. After all, traffic doesn't move until it moves. With a little practice, it was easy to stay in the heart. I appreciated my new levels of energy management as I watched other drivers caught up in mechanical, over-reactive behavior.

If you practice making these "on-the-spot *attitude adjustments*" while experiencing traffic jams, you will get a sneak preview of the difference between *head reactions* and *heart intelligence*. Efficient attitude choices can save you from high-speed stress accumulation.

You can translate this analogy into other real life situations that offer you the same choice: To mechanically act from the *head*, or shift to the wisdom of your *heart* and respond with self-management, efficient action and intelligent solutions.

What is the heart? Well, the physical heart is the pump that circulates the blood through your physical body. But, in referring to the heart, I'm talking about the electrical energy system that surrounds that blood pumping phenomenon. Everyone is aware they have a stomach, and experience what they call solar plexus energy at times. When people are emotionally churning a problem, they often say: "My stomach feels like it's in knots." It's the energy of the solar plexus that surrounds the stomach area that they're experiencing. Everyone knows they have a head, and when the head worries over an issue people often say: "This is giving me a headache."

Your "heart feelings" or "heart sensations" are the energy and activity that surround the heart. Heart energy is a subtle activity that one has to attune to, become aware of and amplify—so that you can understand its significance to you. Your heart sensations give you signals like a traffic light: stop, go, caution. When you feel uncertain, the heart gets mixed in with solar plexus energy, indicating that something needs considering or that there's a fear or insecurity. When your heart signals to you: "Yes, go," it's often accompanied by a more solid, secure feeling inside that's indicating: "This action would be helpful for me, or for someone else or some issue I am dealing with."

Many people credit the brain with producing all these inner signals, thoughts, feelings and energies. The right and left hemispheres of the brain are sophisticated translators of your nonphysical intelligence. The brain is an agent of interpretation and administration, but not the source of your highest intelligence capacity. Neither is the mind. So what source of energy or intelligence would you ascribe to making the brain and mind work or the heart beat? It would have to be a source of more subtle energies and frequencies which science doesn't yet have sensitive enough equipment to measure, though some scientists are making breakthrough progress in this area.

It's logically understood by science that some type of as yet unqualified energy system is responsible for making the heart beat and the brain function. Eventually scientists will be able to measure and understand the electrical content of "spirit." As of today, spirit is mostly referred to in religious or mystical connotations. Many people sense their spirit within. Science will eventually discover the non-physical energy field of spirit and will translate that into plain old streetsense that everyone can understand. This new understanding will be the evidence of higher fourth and fifth dimensional intelligence manifesting into our third dimensional reality (day-to-day consciousness). Don't be one who gives the brain credit for all there is. Then you won't have to backtrack when new evidence is uncovered relative to a higher intelligence that embraces brain/mind capacity.

A system of self-understanding that creates inner peace would be fair to all people and is much needed because most people don't have time to figure out or wait for all the intellectual, scientific formulas. If you learn to attune to your inner wisdom, then you don't have to wait for science to unravel all these understandings to find peace—they will automatically unfold within you.

The traffic jam analogy is simple, yet hopefully effective in helping you understand how the head often reacts unproductively when not managed by *heart* wisdom. Think of the energy wasted daily in Los Angeles and New York through the ongoing stress of traffic jams, and those are just two cities. But the traffic jam is not the issue here. The issue is in understanding that there are two *decision-making modalities* within you—the head and the heart. Many people mechanically make choices from the *head* because they are not yet aware that there's another choice— *heart* intelligence. Heart intelligence works as an efficient guideline for head reasoning.

Without being conscious of your true heart signals, life situations are often perceived just through the head or solar plexus reactions, creating the feelings of knots, insecurities and extreme irritation. The *head* often translates an insecure feeling into a fight or flight reaction, which may not be your most efficient response. If you learn to consciously focus your energies in your *heart* at those times, rather than your head, you can gain a wider perspective and often save yourself much frustration and pain.

Learning how to sense, discriminate and respond to your inner intelligence is a built-in recipe for efficient living. The traffic jam is just a symbol of all the day-to-day situations where the head reacts without the added discrimination of heart intelligence. Enough unmanaged head reactions will reflect themselves in physical depletion and emotional raggedness. Balancing the energy between your *head* and your *heart* creates new energy-saving attitude patterns.

By shifting your focus to your heart feelings during a decision-making process (the place where you often experience common sense and knowingness), you help balance your perceptions and gain a truer picture. For example, when a mother is angry and about to scold a child, she may start to yell...but then she shifts to her heart and re-connects with understanding and compassion, which balances out her response. It takes practice to do it consistently. This is what the book is about: learning to consistently filter your perceptions of life through the heart, thereby saving much energy and preventing continual stress feedback loops.

A new understanding of *heart intelligence* will indicate the advancement of our society and propel us into "common sense" cooperation between people. Remember, it's not the physical head and heart that I'm talking about, but the inner energies and attitudes that are associated with these two areas within the human system. They deal with the thoughts and feelings of your inner self. Most people have noticed times in their lives when they experienced a clear difference between their head thoughts and heart feelings. It's fun observing yourself and becoming more sensitive to the flow of your inner mechanics. You are the captain and maintenance steward of your own ship.

Frequencies—Head and Heart

The intelligence of the heart operates in a different range of frequency bands from that of the head. Let me explain what I mean by "frequency." It's simple: Your consciousness is set up like a radio with different frequency bands. Thoughts and feelings are changeable frequencies just like radio and TV waves. Some of the different frequencies you can experience are: entertainment frequencies, self-care frequencies, pain, sorrow, joy, anger, happiness, social, personal, business and family frequencies. There are a myriad of different frequencies that flow through your thoughts and feelings throughout a day or week. You can learn to change your attitudes and frequencies in the same way that you would turn a radio knob to a different station.

Your *head* frequency bands give you deduction, planning facilitation, calculation, computation, estimation, organization, manipulation—and sometimes self-punishment if you are not careful. Your *heart* frequency bands give you access to care, love, wisdom, intuition, understanding, security, appreciation, etc.— all qualities that people naturally associate with the heart. (Emotions are another range of frequencies which we'll deal with soon.)

For example, if you read this book from just your *head* perspective, you may find yourself thinking at times, "I already read that. It sounds like a repeat." If you read from your *heart*, you can realize that I may be saying similar things but with different colorations, offering a wider intuitive understanding. When writing about thought-provoking subjects, massaging and weaving them from different angles and perspectives often facilitates intuitive assimilation, resulting in a higher-efficiency-ratio of usefulness. People perceive differently, so dealing with levels and layers of sensitive subjects can be extremely important. What's redundant for one can create a deeper level of make-sense and confirmation for another.

Different frequencies of meaning help people connect with new areas of application that could potently effect efficient changes in their lives. Reading from your heart with openness helps activate memory triggers, so that your head can remember the things that count for you. This content is consciously written with care, though vulnerable to controversy and questioning. It's the balance of heart and head frequencies that creates clear perspectives.

The Heart

The intelligence of the heart expresses itself through *intuition*. Some call it an inner voice, some an inner knowing. The heart transmits its intuitive feelings to the head, facilitating a wider, more balanced perspective. People usually think intuition comes from the head; but intuition comes from the heart and the head then helps translate it for practical application to life. (I'll address this more in later chapters.) Without heart intuition, the head often mechanically reacts in non-efficient ways. The head reaction is what creates anxiety, causing you frustration and stress while diluting your system's energy. The heart intuition can take you beyond these typical head reactions that get triggered when things don't go the way you think they should. The intuition is what gives you a wider overview of any situation that you focus upon in day-to-day decision-making—therefore minimizing stress.

When the head is managed by the heart in a joint venture, the results are efficient and productive thoughts and actions. Heart intuition blends the heart qualities (care, security, understanding, sincerity, etc.) with the head's knowledge, igniting the mind's higher functional capacities. You need the head to figure things out, but it's the heart that finally *understands*.

The Head

When I refer to the *head*, I'm talking about the *conglomeration of your mind capabilities*. You would have a hard time getting around without your mind faculties. The *head* is convenient and that's obviously so. A steak knife is convenient and useful, too, but it can be used to stab someone or cut your hand the same way it cuts steak. So the knife is used more efficiently when managed by people, and the *head* is more efficient when managed by the *heart*.

Without heart management, the head can cause much devastation and stress to yourself and others. This can keep repeating throughout the cycle of your life.

Just because the head/mind is a marvel to science doesn't mean that it always acts in your best interest when unmanaged. When not balanced with heart wisdom, your *head* is capable of independently generating frequencies and plans of its own. Hatred, revenge, envy, condescension, greed, arrogance, and many more feelings come from attitudes generated by the *head*—without *heart management*. These attitudes, over a period of time, devitalize your system and surround you with an unseen cloud of mental and emotional pollution. This lingering pollution continues to magnetize more non-efficient thoughts and attitudes. People become victimized by this ongoing process.

The head and heart each have important roles to play in the efficient operation of your total system. When they work harmoniously together, your system can operate at its fullest, most creative potential. Science will eventually be able to measure the difference between head and heart frequencies, since it already acknowledges that everything, brain waves and emotions included, is made of electrical energy.

You have more power to pick and choose your attitudes and perspectives than you may think. You've probably heard people say, "Well, I'll go along with that decision but it's against my better judgment." Your head can often engage in unproductive decisions when your heart is prompting you to do otherwise. Self-empowerment is the progressive ability to consciously manage thoughts and feelings, rather than being mechanically victimized by them.

The *head*, when constantly used by itself, becomes self-centered and gets addicted to stimulation in a way that it can't have peace without it. This causes much of the accumulated stress build-up on the planet—especially in individuals. As you learn to use heart intelligence, you can achieve peace without demanding constant stimulation. Then, when stimulation comes your way, it's an *add-on* but you don't experience a *take-away* when you don't constantly have it. Stimulation can add a healthy "zip" to your life when it's managed by the heart. Without balance and management, the addiction to stimulation can wear down your mental, emotional and physical nature at a high rate of speed.

Drug dependence is merely one form of addiction to stimulation, but an obvious one. Most people are addicted to some type of mental and emotional stimulation, and they accumulate walloping amounts of stress if they don't get enough of their "fix" (like relationship attachments, sports, work, junk food, exercise and umpteen more). All of these ordinary activities can become obvious stimulation addictions, yet there are many, many more subtle and personal addictions that *manipulate* people daily. People are controlled by addictions because they haven't yet learned to integrate heart discrimination with their appetite for stimulation.

Because of the lack of self-security and inner balance, children start the process of stimulation addiction at an early age. For many teenagers, being asked to just stay home and have a family night translates as a jail sentence because of the lack of what they call stimulation—such as partying, sports, shopping, music, dancing, etc. Admittedly, these are fun add-ons, but your level of peace is determined by how you handle yourself when you don't have them. If all televisions went blank for a year, then society would have to face withdrawal symptoms from a serious addiction. TV is fun and informative, but you have to admit it would be nice to know that people could have contentment without depending on TV's perpetual availability.

Fun is fun, but when it turns into attachment and addiction, the "fun value" starts to depreciate. Then what was fun starts to create much more stress than it does enjoyment. For example, sports can be fun, but even a seemingly harmless addiction to watching sports can cause more family problems than people would suspect. Heart-managed stimulation maintains *balance* and *fun* without you becoming over-attached to the experience. You can probably look back over your life and remember lots of situations which started out as fun, but later became a drain and a taxation on your energy and enjoyment. The more you understand how to balance the head activities with heart intelligence, the easier it becomes to eliminate those old self-created stressful patterns—the baggage and luggage in life.

Remember, the *head* is not negative. You need the *head* for thinking, driving, selecting, decision-making, processing data, etc., etc. It's like an endless machine filled with creative potentials and infinite possibilities. Your heart is there as a source of wisdom and bottom-line guidance for the head—in the same way that a mother wisely guides a child, though the child still has flexibility in playing.

When you call on your heart intuition for help, you can be surprised with the facilitation you get—if you listen to it. The problem for many people is that they don't listen to what their heart is trying to tell them. They try to change a *head* attitude by using the *head* to do it. It doesn't work. You end up in the same old rut, time and time again. With sincere practice, you can learn to draw on your own inner strength and bring self-management into areas of your life which you've wanted to manage for a very long time.

The Emotions

People may often sense the promptings of their heart feelings, but repress them because they fear becoming vulnerable. Realize that it's living in the *head* that makes people vulnerable to stress and prone to a profusion of mental and emotional pain. Because the heart frequencies express themselves through feelings, people tend to think of the heart as the emotions. You have probably heard people say, "When I open my heart, people take advantage of me." As you learn more about your heart, you will find that statement to be the opposite of truth. First of all, the *heart consciousness* is not a mushy, wimpy, sweet and defenseless bag of emotions. Your heart *uses* emotions to express its inner wisdom which is translated through feelings of "knowing." *Heart intelligence embraces head intelligence and is the prime, bottom-line strength of your existence.* It represents the real you inside—the essence of the inner child and the responsible adult in a balanced package.

The head often uses emotions to activate insecure feelings in your solar plexus, creating what is called "emotionalism." It's your heart that bails you out after your head runs you aground, especially in the traumatic times of your life. The comfort and security of the *heart* give you the momentum to start anew after exhaustive, self-image disturbances. The *head* keeps crying over spilt milk. The *heart wisdom* helps you appreciate that the "spilt milk" times in your life could have been worse. Bottom line—the heart gives you the strength and understanding to create new self-image attitudes.

The concept of *emotional energy management* will be discussed throughout the book. The emotional nature is where your feelings are registered. Emotions can result from either head or heart thoughts and feelings. A future friend of mine (I haven't yet met him), Hyler Bracey, is the co-author of a book called *Managing from the Heart.* (In a fun and inspiring way, it describes his experiences in learning heart management.) Hyler suggested an interesting twist concerning "feelings" after reading the first draft of this book. He said, "Have feelings—don't let feelings have you." That's a good way of saying, manage your emotions. If you're not in the pilot's seat, they can take you for a wild ride.

The reason the emotions seem hard to manage at times is because they come and go instantly as thoughts or attitudes trigger them—consciously or unconsciously. Emotional energy is not positive or negative, it's neutral—like a car idling. You can press the gas pedal and drive to work responsibly, or you can press the gas and drive a hundred miles an hour into a concrete wall.

The car represents a neutral power that you can use or abuse. Emotional energy is like that.

Emotions add enrichment and excitement to your life. They tremendously increase the texture and the potency of your experience—be it positive or negative. When the emotions are at a low ebb, life can seem bland and fun-less. When they are highly active, you can feel like you're on top of the world if you're enjoying what you're doing. But, if you add emotional energy to thoughts of despondency, you can feel as if you're taking a tour through hell. That's when people do things they later regret, then they remorsefully wonder why they acted that way. The lack of emotional management is a major cause of much swing-shift behavior that people experience.

You often hear people say, "I was having a good time until I lost my temper and exploded." That's like saying you tried to park a car going 70 miles an hour. That's dangerous. It's the head thoughts that get you angry, triggering the emotions and hormones that create temper. Even if temper feels good in the moment, there are a lot of friends lost, rash decisions made, and even deaths caused by unmanaged temper. It's okay to have some feistiness in your system. However, it's important to manage it in a way that you feel at peace with the consequences of your actions.

Often, after a "blow-up" from a head reaction, the energy settles in the heart and you see clearly that reacting wasn't an efficient way to conduct yourself. People often get into guilt trips after emotional blow-outs. A guilt complex is non-efficient—any way you look at it. If you listen to your heart intuition, you gain the insight to apologize or work things out, then you pick up the pieces and go on. It's the head that keeps replaying the situation, reinforcing the guilt or the hurt. The heart can be involved and usually gets the blame for these scenarios, but it's really the head that pilots these situations into non-efficiency and pain.

Repressed Emotions

Repression is not management. It's dangerous and can result in psychological and physical disabilities. Repression is a protective mechanism used by the head when it doesn't have the ability to face or resolve a problem. When the heart feelings are shut down, you don't have the power to release and let go. For example: In many traumatic situations, such as the death of a loved one, child abuse or rape, the heart feelings shut off because of shock and betrayal. You may feel like your heart is broken. The sense of a broken heart results from a head-on collision of broken expectations, broken attachments and a short-circuit of your emotional energy. The heart isn't broken; it's that your heart feelings shut off, and then your emotions run wild or get repressed because of pain, or a sense of loss or remorse.

For long periods of time this can cause a numbness inside which doesn't change until the heart energy re-opens within that individual. The *re-opening* of the heart makes the releasing of repressed emotions possible. The return of feelings often triggers acute head memory of the old pain. Then the unmanaged head mechanically keeps replaying the event. However, by staying centered in the heart, you can more quickly dissolve the subconscious mind tapes that keep reproducing and replaying the painful scenarios. Then you'll be able to clearly perceive that it's really not your heart that re-hashes the hurt, it's your head. As you maintain heart perspective, you accelerate the process of releasing your imprisonment to past events. The heart awareness helps bring the understanding that, no matter what happened, you have the inner power to release and let go—and build anew. If enough of your true self is released through your heart, the re adjustment time is much shorter.

Some would say, yes, but isn't that still a long process? Not if you make direct heart contact and draw from the strength of your spirit within. This connects you with a whole new power accumulator. You can facilitate the heart opening by trying to love and care for more people—any people. Loving and caring for others gives you the incentive to want to clean old repressive patterns out of your data bank. Make sincere efforts from the heart and you'll find the power to manage those old thoughts until they starve from lack of attention. This is the process of self-empowerment. It's heart commitment that gives people the strength to release the old and look forward to the new. Many people experience great lives after releasing traumatic situations.

It could seem as if I don't understand how hard it is. I've been there. I've experienced being shut off in the heart, the repression and the despair. As I regained the deeper heart connection, it made what could have been a long way out much shorter. It doesn't always have to be the long road back from despair. Life goes on, but you can miss it while trying to justify and figure out all the "whys and wherefores" of the past. The re-opening of the heart gives you hope for new possibilities.

You've probably had problems at some point in life where your mind constantly projected the worst-case scenario. Later, simple stepping stones unfolded into efficient solutions and you bypassed all the stressful results that your mind "just knew you were going to go through." If you can get your mind to chill out long enough for your heart to assess any situation, then you can often save the fear and stress accumulation that come from constant worry and anxiety.

As you begin to recognize the difference between the head and the heart inside yourself, you'll see that the unmanaged head approach to life's issues creates most of your stress. Try asking your heart feelings, "What would be the most efficient attitude in this situation?" With practice, you'll become sensitive to inner answers that manifest in a feeling of knowingness. Answers become more clear as you increase your attunement to the way you really feel about things inside. As you learn to manage yourself from the heart, your intuition guides you intelligently through problems. Learn to check in with your heart intuition before acting or reacting, and don't just mechanically sleepwalk through life as many people do.

This book is not intended to inundate you with a profusion of new knowledge. My intention is to share a system that can facilitate you in effectively applying *what you already know within yourself*. The mystery of self-empowerment is in getting yourself to *listen* to your heart feelings, then *acting* on those efficient directives. Self-empowerment is much more than just the achievement of external goals. It's about accumulating the power to efficiently adapt to whatever life brings you. As you peacefully adapt, you magnetize more options for productive solutions and positive changes.

Discovering Common Sense

You don't need to dissect every aspect of the head, heart, and emotions or all the complexities of the brain to uncover the power of your real self. You can drive and manage a car for years without having to be a mechanic—but let's be glad we have them! You can also learn to manage your energies and live a fulfilling life without knowing all the inner workings of the brain. Brain research tremendously facilitates humanity but is not the doorway to the formula for inner peace and human efficiency—although it's part of the puzzle. Heart intuition is the doorway—leading to a *balanced* integration of the head and heart. This balance promotes the development of the whole brain. In future publications, I will address the intricate cybernetics of brain development in relationship to the heart, mind and emotions.

Learning how to access a continuity of common sense can be one of your most efficient accomplishments in this decade. Can you imagine "common sense" surpassing science and technology in the quest to unravel the human stress mess? In time, society will have a new measure for confirming *truth*. It's inside the people—not at the mercy of current scientific methodology. Let scientists facilitate discovery, but not invent your inner truth.

Let me give you an example from my own life of learning common sense (the hard way). It's the story of how I first began to understand the difference between my head and my heart. When I was twenty-two years old, I worked on an assembly line in a furniture factory. I had been with the company for three years with good earnings and had accumulated many benefits. One day my foreman called me into his office. He told me I'd be fired if any more of my work projects were returned from quality control. I was dumbfounded, thinking that my work quality had increased to the maximum rating. Later that afternoon, another worker told me that someone else had slipped the faulty products on my assembly line because of a personal grudge. I visited the boss and enthusiastically relayed the information. He sternly informed me it would be too difficult to prove these allegations. He said that I was still on probation; it was company policy.

My (head) reaction: After work I went home outraged and self-justified. I decided to quit the next day, even without giving notice. The more I thought about how unjust my boss had been, the angrier I got. My ego was bruised and my *mind* was made up. I would show them. "I'll just quit! Let 'em suffer," I thought.

The next morning I was exhausted from processing so much negativity and resentment but was still determined to spite them as planned. However, as I walked to work, my *heart feelings* gave me a completely different perspective on what I should do. I intuited that I should not quit, but should give things time to settle. I realized that the foreman was just looking out for his own job. I could just keep on doing what I'd been doing because I hadn't done anything wrong. I questioned if quitting for revenge was really worth losing the accumulated benefits I'd earned. I loved my job and one incident didn't warrant leaving. Work was hard to find and I had maximum car payments plus rent and grocery bills.

"Maybe I should just chill out." I pondered, "Maybe it's more efficient to make peace with this situation rather than launch war—therefore coming out way better in the long term." That was my *heart* talking.

By the time I reached the factory, I was well aware of having two choices: 1) Quit the job—show them, but good! 2) Make peace with the situation, knowing that it would probably work out. That's what I was really feeling in my heart.

So, guess what happened when I arrived at work? I felt good and had made an inner decision to stay with the company. That seemed right, considering all aspects of the issue. But because of being in deep contemplation, I was two minutes late getting to my work station and the foreman promptly reprimanded me in front of several people. I was embarrassed and got angry all over again. I conveniently forgot the heart decision to keep the job and QUIT!—right on the spot. I pranced macho style to the office, collected my pay and was outta there.

On the way home I stopped for a soda and bragged to the store clerk about how good it had felt to tell them I quit and how I'd really shown them. Being wise, he didn't see the victory in my story.

Conclusion: A victory it was not. By evening, everything within me realized that the choice I had made was non-efficient. When I went back to the factory, they were quick to tell me that I couldn't have my job back. It took two months to finally find another job and I lost my car as well, not to mention the other stress that accumulated from the inconvenience.

I experienced all of this in the name of *principle*. Be cautious when you are using the word principle to justify your actions or decisions concerning important choices in life. Many times, when you defend *the principle of something*, it's only your head taking a stance because it feels good at the moment, but doesn't make for good later.

The irony of the story is that I had already realized my heart's decision and was going to go with that. Then, because of the lack of self-management or self-empowerment, I emoted and reverted back to a head decision, and you know the rest of the story. I accumulated a megaton of stress because of a non-efficient energy expenditure.

This incident was valuable because it gave me a fiery desire for the power to manage my energies and to follow through with my heart feelings, especially when they were so obvious. As I practiced, I soon developed the sensitivity to easily identify the difference between a heart or head directive, especially when they were not in sync. Heart directives are what you often, deep inside, already know to be the best course of action. Once you can see the difference between your *head* and your *heart*, you accumulate more power to follow through with your heart intuition. After you've made a heart choice, your whole system naturally feels better. You realize you've done what's right for you, not just what you impulsively wanted to do in the moment (as I did when I walked out on that job).

Your fun in living increases as you eliminate and prevent stress by practicing the management of your day-to-day life from the *heart*. This is a system about you and yourself. You don't have to graduate from a course of enlightenment to benefit from self-truth. You benefit immediately as you start to bypass the mind processors which so often override the heart intuition—even when your heart may be screaming at you to make a different decision.

Have you ever walked through the woods or on the beach, feeling good and self-connected—then declared to yourself that you needed to make some personal changes, especially in the areas of mental or emotional management? Then, did you make a pledge to yourself saying, "Starting this very day, things are going to be different because now, at last, I am going to take charge of my life, and eliminate that excess stress that drags me around the block daily!"? (You know, like getting unattached from a draining relationship, completing a diet you started five times, overcoming financial worries, etc.) Then, did you go home and practice your new commitment through that night, but wake up the next day and go for months with only a vague memory of that pledge you made? (Like people do each New Year's.)

The answer is possibly "yes" in many cases. Why is it so easy to forget pledges concerning self-management? It's because people don't consider managing their thoughts and emotions until they overload on stress. Then they are forced to go to their hearts for a self-talk in hopes of finding some release. If you learn to attune to your heart feelings while making decisions throughout the day, you avoid the stress overload that results in emotional setbacks. When you get emotionally drained, physical ailments often follow and 'round and 'round life goes. You can get off the exhausting merry-go-rounds in life as you experience the efficiency and integrity of your own inner strength.

Another Common Sense Analogy

Here's another day-to-day analogy on the head and the heart. Let's try a Dick and Jane story: Jane heard, through the grapevine, that her girlfriend's husband, Dick, had said she wasn't quick-minded enough to be his bridge partner. To say the least, Jane's vanity was destroyed by this remark. "How dare you judge me!" she thought, while feeling the temperature of her anger rise. She wanted to tell Dick where to get off, that she knew he wore a toupee, that his uncut lawn made the rest of the neighborhood look like a garbage dump, etc., etc. (head reaction with amped up emotions).

During the next week, Jane couldn't get Dick's remark off her mind and the anger and resentment escalated. She excused herself from the next bridge game, though she really enjoyed playing. Next, she canceled her tickets to a banquet, just because Dick was supposed to be there. By now she had a three-story-condo-resentment going because she blamed Dick for her missing the bridge game and the banquet, and for the painful comment that he had made. "Stuff happens," doesn't it! (Still *head* and emotional reactions so far.)

Finally, Dick's wife, Sally, called Jane and said, "Girl, we have to talk." Reluctantly, yet starving for release of any kind, Jane met Sally. She had a good shoulder cry as they confirmed endearments to each other. This helped Jane release and re-connect with her heart, giving her a clearer perspective.

Conclusion: After Jane got back into her heart awareness, she realized that:

1) She overreacted because of self-image-rejection and then blew things out of proportion.

2) It would have been more energy-efficient (she wouldn't have suffered so much) if she had confronted Dick, rather than reacting in a way that inevitably causes stress to accumulate.

3) Her snowballing (head) reactions compounded *her* misery while attempting to spite Dick.

4) In her heart, she really did love Dick (and thought his hairpiece was becoming and actually cute).

So, she had a heart-to-heart talk with Dick and all went well. He apologized sincerely and, as Dick and Jane stories go, it all worked out.

The list, 1 through 4, indicates how your perceptions can totally change after you re-connect with your heart feelings. Learning the difference between your head and your heart helps you attune to intuitive solutions at the onset of problems—before you waste so much energy through emotional *head reactions*. Remember, emotional energy is neutral. It will increase head reactions as well as heart feelings.

The story ended well. And in a short period of time. But realize this: Many people, in similar situations, go for years carrying baggage from past resentments and never make any attempt to work them out. When old negative patterns are not released from your system, they are stored in the subconscious and can constantly dilute your energies without you even being aware of the process.

It could amaze you to know how much energy it takes to maintain a resentment over a period of time, and how much it drains and ages your system. Yes, I said *ages* your system! Stress acts as a booster pack to the standard biological aging process. If your mental and emotional energies are out of phase with your *heart* long enough, your physical body will finally catch the residual effects.

Resentments create much stress, but they feel good to people at times—at least for the moment. At times being drunk on alcohol may feel good in the moment, too, but taxes often have to be paid later. The tough part about resentments is that the people holding resentments usually suffer more than the ones they are resenting. It's just more efficient to release and let go, forgive, or work it out. It's your tail you save when you make the efficient choices. Resentment is an "energy vampire" that quickly relieves you of your youth—any way you stack it!

By now, I hope you are gaining a more sensitive understanding of the difference between the heart and the head. Most people already have some understanding of what their *heart feelings* are. I'm only trying to assist you in **remembering them** by offering these simplified approaches. You can benefit immediately with very little practice. It would just make *streetsense* that a true system of efficiency, awareness, and stress reduction would be inherent within each person. Personal growth is about the development of that empowerment within your own self. It's finally **you** who has to look after **yourself** and doctor your own "stress mess." And it's you who procrastinates the process.

When people ask of life, "Where's the Beef?"—they are really asking, "Where is the hope for mental and emotional management within the individuals in our society?" Let's wake up and realize that it's the lack of mental and emotional management that keeps the *stress monster* alive and thriving as we operate under the illusion of intelligent living standards. All the evidence of increasing stress is proof that we don't operate from intelligent living standards. We are growing into that understanding, but not by the merits of high-tech achievement. High-tech and science are applauded advancements of the *mind*, yet they can create *illu-*

sions concerning the true advancement of humanity.

The advancement of our society will be indicated by a much more peaceful *cooperation* and *communication* within all people systems, and especially within oneself. This achievement will come about as a result of new breakthroughs in the areas of intuitional development. Intui-Technology will prove to be our most profitable future research investment. (More about this in CHAPTER 4.) Stress will produce the pressures to bring about this new advancement in the not-too-distant future.

Exploring how to become more attuned to the intuitive voice in your heart *will benefit the whole* more than landing on Mars and the planting of another vanity flag. A Mars walk could be fun, but at this time we need to invest in a technology that will help people have a more peaceful "street" walk on *this* planet.

People already know that heart feelings feel better and more complete than unmanaged head reactions. As you manage life from the heart, the energy of stress is transformed into quality experience. This management is easier than you may think if you give it the same focused attention that you would learning a new hobby. Practicing heart attunement is the key. It's a common sense approach to stress management. A streetsense strategy.

Many people muster the power to practice music or sports six hours a day, yet they may not have the power to resist becoming mentally and emotionally drained by a boss's comments or a five o'clock traffic jam. People are always searching for the power of external conveniences. The real power that would profit you the most is the power to manage unorganized energy patterns that drain you on a regular basis. Self-empowerment begins with the patching of your energy leaks followed by preventive maintenance.

Now, let's look at a head and heart paradox that applies to society at large. It's about the many thousands of people busting their tails in ambitious pursuits to become something that their *hearts* would not have chosen. Since society doesn't encourage people to listen to their *heart* directives, *head ambition* compels them to slave towards goals that may not bring their highest peace and happiness—and especially fun in living.

Many children feel socially pressured into certain professions, like becoming a doctor, lawyer, scientist, etc. Giving wholesome encouragement to children in vocational guidance is prudent, yet teaching them to listen to their *hearts* at an early age will give them the awareness to make intuitive choices of their own. How can adults teach a younger generation something they haven't learned or practiced themselves? That's an interesting dilemma because adults think children are out of hand, while children think adults have an outdated understanding. Who's right? Often they both are, but ponder what causes this stand-off. It's because inner development and self-truth have been side-stepped for the glorification of vanity achievements and external ambitious pursuits. Children suffer especially from this type of societal programming.

The Importance of Sincere Communication

The lack of heart communication constantly increases the gap between younger and older generations. It's obvious that children seem to be born today with an extreme innate awareness and mental quickness. Confusion in communication between the generations is on the increase—and without a lot of hope or solutions being offered. However, when adults and children alike learn to communicate and make decisions from their heart sensitivity, then the so-called "communication gap" will dispel itself. Technology and science alone cannot create the remedy for this social quandary; it will have to be dealt with through individual self-awareness and responsibility.

Eventually, society will realize the necessity of incorporating the understanding of *heart and head management* into education at all levels. This can do much to reduce the rising high school drop-out rate, not to mention the growing epidemics of teenage pregnancy, alcohol abuse, suicide, and more. The point I'm intending to stir is that it's the lack of heart connection (or deeper connection with their spirit) that has caused many youngsters and adults to end up misplaced and unhappy.

Following heart directives may not be the "instant" panacea for bridging the generation or communication gaps among people, yet it will be one of the first advanced initiatives proposed. As you personally ponder the situation, you can intuitively realize that it's the *heart connection* that has been missing all along—with oneself and with others.

When communication is approached from the heart, you experience sincerity and resonance. Without the heart engaged, communication can be dry and dull—and you can't wait to get away for a break. Have you ever noticed workplaces where people seem to co-exist in a mechanical, robotic way, without much sincerity or care in their communications? It's like being in a sleepwalking environment. The absence of heart energy sterilizes an environment.

The heart is not just for bailing you out of problems. It's especially good for *preventing* problems. It's a source of strength and commitment, adding quality and buoyancy to your relationships or activities. You can notice the difference in the quality of a lecture or a talk when it is given from the heart with sincerity. People tell each other to play and sing from the heart. This brings another level of obvious quality and texture to their performance.

People know what heart promptings feel like in different situations (such as the feeling that gives you the urge to show someone appreciation, or the feeling that tells you not to take that third drink, or to release old resentments). As you get more familiar with those promptings and listen, your heart intelligence unfolds, giving you moment-to-moment self-management in all situations in life. Remember, when the head is not in a joint venture with the heart, you can make decisions that you may regret, resulting in more stress than efficiency.

If you're not sure what your heart is telling you, write down your feelings and thoughts concerning a situation on a piece of paper. Then try to read them objectively and see which make the most common sense—or save you the most energy and leave you the most satisfied with yourself. As heart intuition becomes more active in your life's agenda, you're more likely to discover common sense solutions in most decision-making processes.

Don't get frustrated with your first efforts to decipher which are your heart feelings. After a few days of self-listening, you'll start to recognize the intuitive feelings—and more easily distinguish them from the scattered, unmanaged mind chatter or the emotional, solar plexus reactions. As you practice this process, it soon becomes automatic. As it becomes automatic, it facilitates the integration of your *spirit* (the most fulfilling and fun manifestation of your real self) into your day-to-day life.

This is not a book endorsing any particular religion. It's addressed to all people and written with caring intentions not to interfere with anyone's perceptions of who or what God is or isn't. I respect all people's right to believe in whatever spiritual source they choose that resonates within their heart. Those beliefs are very personal and have to be decided within one's own heart. Though I refer to heart intelligence and its effectiveness in self-management, that doesn't mean that I don't acknowledge and respect a higher power. I have proven to myself (as have others) that managing my energies from the heart creates a more intelligent and deeper personal connection with the higher power or source of love.

What I am suggesting is that your heart is the likely human point of connection to your true spirit, highest self, higher power, the Light, or God. If you direct your life from the heart with sincerity, it can help you manage your energies to make a cleaner, clearer connection with your higher source. It's a sensitive subject, but I'll try to explain my perceptions of the heart without stepping on anyone's toes. My intention is to address all the people in providing a system of day-to-day facilitation for self-understanding, allowing them the inalienable right to choose their own spiritual resources.

During my practice of managing from the heart, I was awakened to the realization that "You can help yourself." I realized that helping yourself facilitates a higher connection with your spirit, and spirit then facilitates you in helping yourself. It becomes a joint venture that makes sense. Self-empowerment is the process of learning to manifest your true self in your day-to-day life. To me, a gift from the higher power would be to give human individuals a blueprint of how to grow more into the likeness of that source of power and intelligence. From my experience, self-empowerment would be such a gift. Heart intelligence unfolds the blueprint—the gift of how "You can help yourself."

The intuition that flows through the heart comes from higher intelligence via the source. Your heart is a convenient trunkline for connecting to the highest qualities of your spirit within. People innately associate the following words with the heart—Strength, Courage, Sincerity, Compassion, Patience, Peace, Fairness, Care, Truth—and especially Love. These words are verbal cages surrounding powerful energies, or heart frequencies, which can transform your mental and emotional perspectives, bringing them into balance. As you engage the power of heart attitudes (courage, patience, sincerity, etc.) they act as *anti-stressperants*.

Wouldn't it be convenient to have the "essence" of patience, peace, or courage in a bottle—spray it on in the morning to protect yourself from daily attitude slumps! This sounds zany. However, in learning to follow your intuitive heart feelings, you create healing and regenerative attitudes that become a way of life. Attitudes generated from the heart are your convenient, built-in, common sense tools for stress reduction. Remember, with a little practice of listening to your own heart, it doesn't take long to prove this system to yourself.

3

Care and Overcare
The Stressful Difference
Between Them

When *care* becomes **overcare**, it creates an ongoing deficit in your mental, emotional and physical health! Why? Because *overcare* drains and depletes your system. *Overcare* keeps people from truly enjoying and benefiting from the things they *care* about. Once overcare sets in, you soon have attachment; over-attachment weaves you into a web of emotional vulnerability and you set yourself up to be hurt, disappointed, and drained.

I'm not just talking about over-attachment to people. I'm talking about over-attachment to issues, attitudes, places, things, opinions, ideas, environments, sports, entertainment, etc., etc., etc. *Overcare* dilutes your energy anywhere it is spent. It's great to *care* and we should strive to do that. However, it's intelligent to learn where to draw the line.

Listening to your deeper heart feelings can help you discriminate the difference between care and overcare; then your energy expenditures become more profitable and less draining. The *head* is what gets people caught up in overcare and attachment, yet most people think it is their *heart* that causes this. It's not! This is one of the most slippery illusions in human psychology. The heart cares, but it's the *head* that takes that care into *overcare*. Learning self-management can bring this into balance.

To come into your own self-empowerment, you first have to assess the energy leaks in your system, then stop them. Period. *Overcare* ranks close to the top of the list of human energy drains. It's in the same family as worrying, and worrying hasn't won you many trophies. Here's a common example of *overcare* to give you a "hands-on" understanding.

Many parents have a hard time emotionally releasing their children when they leave home, go to college, get married, etc. They spend much time worrying about their children's welfare and suffering from a sense of loss. This often leads to a smothering involvement with their offspring as they are trying to get on with their own lives.

Much ongoing stress is created in these overly-attached relationships. The parents stay stressed because of their overcare; the children stay stressed because of their parents' over-involvement in their affairs. Not only is it hard for some parents to release young adults to live their own lives, they often want to govern the lives of their grandchildren as well. It all originates from care—but, when it crosses the line into overcare, the family relationships get drained. Everybody thinks that everyone else is wrong. This can lead to family fussing, fighting, feuds and separation.

So, the stress perpetuates year after year, all in the name of *care*. It's *overcare*—a lack of balance in releasing and letting go. It's wonderful to love and care—but the overcare blocks the pathways of love, becoming a hindrance and a continuing source of stress to all concerned. This is not an attack on concerned parents and I am not saying that parents shouldn't care. I'm talking about the need for *balanced* caring.

I have experienced similar quandaries in life, in which it was hard for me to let go so others could grow. Stressful? Yes. Still, by gaining a deeper heart perspective, I learned to care for people, but not overcare to the point that it caused stress from interference. As I released my attachments to helping people, my care became more effective.

Care has strength. It can help. *Overcare* bleeds your strength and can eventually exhaust the people you are (over) caring for. Why keep putting yourself through the wringer, when you tell yourself constantly that you're not going to do it again? That's your heart telling you to stop overcaring! After you get more sensitive to following your heart guidance, you will efficiently balance your over-attachments, allowing people the same freedom to experience growth as you demand for yourself.

Overcare is a human condition, a social dis-ease, and most have experienced it. You find overcare in different degrees— concerning people, places, things, issues, attitudes, vanities, etc., etc. As you understand its disguises, you will realize the hundreds of ways that people overcare *daily* throughout the planet. If you calculated the energy lost and the distortion created by the millions of people who overcare in just one day, the energy deficit would amaze you. What a waste when it all started with *care*— care that became unmanaged.

That accumulated distortion doesn't just vanish. It looms throughout the planet and feeds the "stress monster" that constantly victimizes the masses of people. The stress monster knows that enough people will live non-efficiently each day, so that it can grow in power while feeding off their ignorance. Maybe you can't stop others from feeding it, but you don't have to contribute to the process. Just practice self-management by sincerely listening to your inner voice.

How? You can have a self-talk and review your involvements with people, places, attitudes, issues, etc. Then, attune to your heart feelings to see if you are *overcaring* about things when you should be just *caring*. With a sincere approach, you'll be surprised to find wasted energy in many areas due to overcare. Make note of them because overcare is slippery. Make efforts not to keep repeating the same stress-creating patterns. The more energy leaks you stop, the less stress you incur. The less stress you incur, the more quality you get out of any experience. It's a simple game of economy. Use your energy efficiently by listening to your heart and learning to follow its intuitive directives.

Through practicing and remembering, you begin to recognize overcare at the onset. Then focus your energies in your heart and just say no. Adults tell children to "just say no" but often find it hard to do themselves. As you understand this chapter, you may become increasingly aware of certain energy drains in your life caused by overcare. You might say, "I know I'm overcaring in some areas, but I can't seem to stop it." People often fail in their efforts to change deep-rooted patterns. This is because their efforts are made from the head, without the power of the heart. *Head* efforts create novelty and then they fizzle out, leaving you feeling like a failure with a flimsy constitution. At times you can block overcare with the conscious mind, but the emotions maintain a state of irritation because the overcare is still programmed in the subconscious mind. If you make efforts sincerely from the *heart*, rather than the head, then you release the overcare from the subconscious as well as stabilize the emotions.

Heart power behind affirmations is always more effective in changing subconscious electrical patterns. Some people repeat affirmations for weeks from the head, but if done a tenth of that time from the heart, it would have a more dynamic effect on changing non-efficient attitudes and increasing inner strength. Remembering to engage the heart feelings is important. The *sincere desire* for management adds fire to the *remembering process*.

Once you realize how much stress you can accumulate in one day from *overcaring* (and then multiply that by 365), you'll want to make efforts to bring your *care* into balance. Self-imposed stress can make you feel aged, weary and tired. Managing overcare closes up energy leaks in your system, one by one, which is a common sense strategy for stress management.

True *heart* efforts generate a continuity of strength, leading to completion and inner satisfaction. If you don't always get expected results, there could be a good reason. Practice connecting with the inner strength of your heart for the understanding to see things through.

Steps to Managing your Overcare

So, what else can you do to keep your care from crossing over the line into overcare? First, start watching yourself daily for signs of overcare concerning people, issues, attitudes or events. Then, observe the overcare which causes you stress when life doesn't seem to accommodate you. Assess where you might over-identify or be overly attached to issues or other people's approval. Write down some of your areas of overcare and become more conscious of them.

Next, begin noticing how long you mentally chew on things in your spare time that are already "spilt milk" and need to be wiped out of your focus of attention. Check to see if you have a lot of grudges or resentments. That's another type of overcare that drains people of much of their energy.

When you're trying to help people, don't cry in their beer with them. It doesn't help. It just makes you both more "pitiful" the next morning. Stress and the "burn-out syndrome" will decrease as people practice bringing more balance into their care for others. Realize there are many changes people could make for the better, if they weren't victimized by *overcare*. Have the heart to help people but learn when to let go and let grow.

Remember, your *head* creates the overcare, while your *heart* creates the balanced care. At any moment, you can go to your heart and ask, "Is my caring truly efficient? Is it helpful for both myself and the other?" Be honest with yourself. Your heart intuition will guide your discrimination as you practice using it.

Learning to *care more sincerely* about other people, and yourself, is at the top of the list for efficient self-maintenance. Care regenerates and heals; overcare depletes your energy reserve, often diluting your desire to care any more.*

To operate a car without oil in the pistons is equivalent to a human living a life without *care* in his or her system. True care is a frequency, or feeling, that radiates from your heart. It flows through your system and lubricates your thought and feeling nature, while decreasing friction and resistance in your life. Care not only acts as a mental and emotional detergent within your system, it also adds quality and texture to your relationships with people and all issues.

Remember, I'm not just talking about overcaring in relationship to people. It could be overcaring about a new car that you know is costing you too much money and therefore stress. It could be overcaring about politics, abortion laws, religion, race, Russia, etc., etc. When people get "too caught up" and over-identified with social issues, often they end up creating more stress for themselves and the planet. It's unfortunate, especially when the original purpose of their mission was to relieve planetary stress and create more peace. Peace marches motivated from anger and overcare may seem effective in the short run. But, demonstrations and marches that exemplify peace and balanced care, while maintaining firm intentions, will effect more beneficial changes for the planetary whole in the long run.

Social Care

It's especially okay to *care* and get involved in social concerns. Yet, *overcare* in the name of peace averts many of the good-willed intentions, therefore creating more of a "stress-mess" for the

---

*A controlled study on care-giving among nurses (Montgomery 1990) observed that it wasn't caring that led to burn-out, but the lack of caring. The study reported that, "caring itself allows nurses to access a very important source of energy and renewal."

whole. Saving the whales and saving the trees are important, as long as we realize that *a deeper caring for other people and learning self-management* could be ten times more important to the whole of society for producing peace and harmony.

At this point in time, people as a whole care more for issues, things, money, etc., than they do for each other. Society is learning the hard way that the lack of care and respect for each other causes the ecological and political systems to fall short of balance and efficiency. I'm talking about the lack of care that exists country to country, state to state, town to town, among businesses, within churches, within families, and within individuals for themselves.

All areas of relationship are experiencing compounded stress because they have lost contact with the heart frequency of care amidst business and social interactions. Governments and businesses use people as pawns to develop self-centered ambitions, forgetting that care, cooperation, and co-creation would produce more harmony, balance and success for the whole.

The heart's not just some mushy and sentimental doormat. It especially has business bands of common sense and discrimination, meaning: You don't have to lay down and let people take advantage of you without looking out for yourself. If you do that, you end up blaming the negative results on the heart, when your unmanaged head reactions caused the stress feedback. Don't let the head shut off your caring if other people don't respond as you hoped they would. Go back to your heart and find another common sense approach—it could be to simply move on. Just remember, heart intelligence has crisp, clear business discrimination. Use it.

In the next decade, large numbers of people will affirm that the *heart* is what's missing in all the social institutions that fashion our lives. Signs of this are already apparent in news releases, and major magazines often feature articles that suggest that *family ambience* is a key missing ingredient in business, religions and social movements. The family frequency band of care is missing in the core of planetary interactions and involvements, and excess stress is the reverberating consequence. (More about family in CHAPTER 6.)

Is it surprising to read about *overcare* for a few paragraphs and then about *not enough care* in the paragraphs that follow? It sounds like a cross frequency, yet it's not. It's simply that people care too much about the nonessentials and too little about things that count. The planet is toxic with stress because of the *lack of true care* and the distortions from *overcare*. This seriously affects the planetary balance as evidenced in the rain forests and the ozone layer. People eventually will realize that distortions in consciousness affect the rhythms of nature. They will recognize the need to clean up the *inner-ecology* (the giant mental and emotional oil spill). As people clean up their inner ecology, they will intuit more efficient directions to balance the outer ecology.

From my perspective, the next decade will produce enough stress to cause mass reconsideration of the *effects* that negative, non-caring thoughts and actions have on our (future) ecosystem. (This is not a doomsday type prediction; it's just an obvious trend projection based on the present lack of individual energy management.)

The lack of care and harmonious interaction between countries and people has always had an adverse effect on the natural rhythms of the planet. It's just that now, the deficit accrued from non-efficient thinking and living is releasing a backwash of increased "people stress" into the entire system. The planet is not being punished; it's not a personal thing. It's just a mathematical effect from a cause. Stress is not retribution. It's simply inharmonious incoming energy created by non-efficient outgoing energy— a cause and effect kind of thing.

For many people, harmonious living sounds like a pipe dream or a non-approachable idealism. By harmony, I'm not implying that within a few years everyone will be giving each other foot massages and the shirts off their backs. Still, life can get much better than it is if individuals practice self-responsibility. As people relate more from the heart, the planetary equilibrium can be re-established. Again, it's just math—efficiency outgoing produces more harmony incoming. You don't have to wait for the rest of the planet to find balance before *you* can have your peace, fun and quality in life. *Practice loving and caring for people more.* You enjoy it when it comes your way. It's the way of the heart and can tremendously help clean up the internal stress environment. Planetary equilibrium readily responds to the balance or the lack of balance in the people. As people love each other more, they develop more of a natural tendency to extend that love to the Earth and all aspects of creation. Everything is nurtured as it experiences love.

When people live for years in the head, it upsets their psychic equilibrium which is the result of not enough heart energy flowing through their system. When heart energy is scarce in your system, you tend to develop crystallized patterns in your physical, emotional and mental natures. Mental rigidity keeps you stuck in ruts, seriously hampering your ability to adapt to new situations. When adaptability is low, your immune system suffers. Many illnesses can and do develop from these patterns. But that's not all. You miss the quality of life day-to-day and moment-to-moment that you could have had by loving and caring more.

Remember: Care is your engine oil, the lubricant that slows down the aging process because it keeps your mental and emotional nature flexible and filled with *spirit*. Once you start losing contact with your spirit, life gets dusty and pale. "Is it worth it?" you wonder at times. If you ever suffer from lack of spirit and feel that you are just living and operating on raw *nerve* energy, then practice loving and caring for people at deeper, more sincere levels. *Care* flowing through your system will gradually re-connect you with your *spirit* and *vitality*.

Your *spirit* houses your fun and zip in life. Yet, because of excess stress in the game of life, many people hardly experience their "vitality and sprite" and feel lucky to get through a week without croaking. This is what I mean by living on *nerve* energy, which is unnatural since it creates "dues" to be paid. Learning to follow your heart will *naturally* integrate the flow of your spirit into your entire system. You just have to care enough for **you** to do this for yourself.

Research has often evidenced the power of love and care in the process of self-healing. So, preventive maintenance would be to practice generating more *love* and *care* energy consistently. You can do this by living more from your heart intelligence which is naturally designed for self-maintenance and creative living.

Within your heart, you connect with the most trustworthy counselor you can depend on when the bottom falls out in different areas of life. People chase systems of peace, but they are only effective to the degree that they help you contact your real heart truth. Your heart is your personal built-in discriminator. Don't just use it for picking up the pieces when tragedy strikes. Use it daily to become more efficient in all things. This doesn't mean that heart power can make the noisy traffic in New York disappear. You can use that inner power to make *peace* with the traffic and adapt to it—then it might even be fun.

There's a lot to be said for "learning to make peace with issues," especially if you can't change them right away. For example: Adapting to the recent large earthquakes in California had to be extremely stressful for the people immediately involved. It was a stress they couldn't control so they had to either adapt the best they could or experience mental distress. Psychologists observed people who shared similar losses, but noticed extreme differences in their psychological adjustment times. They also observed some who had minor losses experiencing extreme overcare and distress, while others who lost much were caring and appreciative that they had their lives and experienced minimal stress. How is it that some people seem to adjust and adapt much more quickly than others? It's the heart security that helps you to quickly adapt in a crisis and re-establish mental and emotional equilibrium.

When people use only their *minds* to adapt after a crisis or a trauma, it can take longer because they find themselves constantly replaying the painful memories and mentally itemizing all the things they lost. This is normal for a while because of the human reaction to shock. However, if you allow this *overcare* to continue unchecked, you destroy your peace in this moment as well as diminish your chances for peace in the future. It's your heart security and power that can get you out of the same old mental rut. The aging process is not necessarily hastened by the problems people have—it's accelerated by the non-efficient ways people deal with those problems.

Don't say "yeah but," "yeah but." Just build a sincere relationship with your inner heart directives and you can turn an "upside down world" back over again, making it even better in the future. Many people have stumbled onto this realization and have proven it true. You don't have to stumble onto it; you can *consciously* create inner peace and make attitude adjustments by managing your energies. Make sustained efforts and not just frustrated attempts. It's you who has to draw the line between care and overcare, then release and let go of non-efficient attitudes and mind processors. The only distance between you and accomplishing this is *sincere* practice.

I repeat: **Care** oils and regenerates your system as you practice caring for others or for yourself. **Overcare** drains your system, leaving you to operate on nerve energy, diluting your health and the quality of your life—especially the fun factor. Practice observing yourself and you can weed the *overcare* out of your life, adding quality and vitality to your experiences.

*A Footnote:

Upon hearing about the heart system of self-empowerment, some people commented that it sounded too easy and asked, "Where's the catch?" The only catch is whether you sincerely practice or not. If managing from the heart seems idealistic, then familiarity can warm your perspective. A hundred years ago, people watching birds fly overhead would have thought a three hundred passenger airplane was idealistic. If you re-read the book and put into practice, step-by-step, that which resonates with you, then you'll discover the truth of the heart for yourself and experience new levels of self-management. Example—if at first you only benefit from changing your attitude in some of the inconveniences of life, like traffic jams, or in minor irritations with friends, family, co-workers, etc., that's one step of the way which can save you much energy and stress accumulation over time. Then if you practice: learning to create a joint venture between your head and your heart, learning not to overcare, developing a deeper sincerity in your relationships with people, and utilizing the other techniques found in each chapter—your whole system will feel better from the energy you save and the vitality you gain. At times you may take three steps forward and fall back two but don't judge yourself. Jump right back in the game. It's rewarding, and many people are successfully using the system. It's a "you on you" adventure.

Intui-Technology:
A New Dimension of Efficiency

Humanity should be complimented for the widespread conveniences which were borne from the many technological breakthroughs over the past few hundred years. Technology gives us convenience which is our assumed proof of efficiency in life. People have an innate desire for convenience. Notice how self-rewarding it is to buy something on sale, talk the price down on an item, or negotiate a better deal for your company. You get excited because it seems as if you've done something *efficient*. Often, the "rush" of getting a deal seems worth more than the money saved.

However, you can pride yourself your whole life for having the knack of being productive, *while actually being extremely non-efficient and non-effective in the areas of your life that really count.* The evidence of this on a mass level is the stress "backwash" that we experience on the planet. So new computer chips, electric cars, or a walk on Mars prove only one kind of advancement (surface level), not the kind that can "bail" us out of the *stress* we experience in family, business, social, political, religious, and self-relationships.

It will take another kind of advanced technology to achieve the seemingly invincible task of evolving the efficiency and integrity of human communication (the task of de-stressing human relationship patterns). I call the advanced technology for stress dissipation Intui-Technology™: the systematic unfoldment of the intuition—the technology of *inner-efficiency*. That's the technology in which we need to make new "breakthroughs." Mental and emotional energies interplay so forcefully in your system that *intuition* is needed to bring them into balanced expression.

As the inner voice is amplified through the practice of listening to your heart feelings, intuition naturally unfolds. As you make *sincere* efforts to unfold your intuition, it can develop more quickly than you may think. "Then why don't the masses of people have more intuition if it's so simple?" you might ask. Here's why. People tend to approach intuitive development from the head, and not the heart. That's why it remains such a mystery at the present level of human understanding.

The heart gives voice to the intuition if you learn to listen and apply its free wisdom. In religion and philosophy, they call it "the still small voice," or people say, "listen to what your heart tells you." Both are referring to intuition, yet people still try to find it from a head approach. They think intuition is a flash inside the head that releases wisdom. Intuition from the *heart* sends illumination to the *head* center, then the head flashes with knowingness and facilitates in manifesting the idea or realization. That's why it *seems* like the head gives birth to intuition, yet the frequency band of intuition enters your system through the heart, from your source of light and understanding. The heart quickly transmits the intuition to the head, which acts as a *substation* of the heart. Your heart is the mainframe "intelligence center" in your system.

Intuitional development can facilitate all areas of human activity, even your day-to-day routine decision-making. Many people think that intuition is only useful for discoveries, such as the invention of the light bulb or a "flash" that gives you the winning lottery numbers, etc. Yes, it has to do with that, but that's only one slice of a larger pie of possibilities. Intuition can be just as efficient in directing relationship problems, business affairs, social affairs, managing your time, the way you dress, the way you eat, and on and on. It provides you with the *directions* for effective unfoldment in any given area of focus. Intuitive development can make all areas of your life more productive—and therefore much more enjoyable and complete.

You don't have to discover another "light bulb" to verify an intuitive experience. You've experienced heart feelings before, signaling you to change attitudes or go in certain directions—that's intuition coming through. Your intuition can prompt you not to blow your top or over-react with children, family, business disappointments, etc. It can offer you efficient guidance in simple or complex situations. It will develop to the degree of your efforts; that's fair. As you practice following the heart, your intuition becomes more user-friendly and accessible. You'll find intuition much more accessible if you don't put the word on a pedestal making it too complex to approach.

Intuitive research has to expand past the *head center* (mind/brain) approach, or it will result in only limited discoveries. Science will eventually break through to the realization that intuition can be accessed easily through an individual's *heart* contact, which then engages the head for facilitation and completion.

The masses are in need of simple packages of understanding. That's all they have time for. And that's what intuition is famous for—efficiency in a simple package. Everyone has the capacity to recognize and develop their inner knowingness. Listen more deeply to your inner truth and you can prove this to yourself. What's wrong with a little practice for such a lucrative return?

Earlier, I implied that modern technology has made life more convenient. And I also suggested that technology still hasn't offered much that would create more efficiency in the management of your mental and emotional energy expenditures. You need a technology that can offer solutions for: why children carry weapons to the classroom; why we still have wars; why people have to be scared to go out of their houses at night; why people are allowed to starve when there is plenty; why many families can't get along with each other, much less the rest of the world; why there is more crime, more rape, more violence, etc., etc., etc. It's time for inner-technology. Intui-Tech research will focus on these pressing social issues.

Stress overloads in our society prove that psychoanalysis is not equipped to offer the needed solutions. It's time for a new twist on an old subject—psychology. It's obvious that there's something missing in humanity's approach to relationship problems. *Accessing the intuition through deep heart connection leads to the development of inner strength, and that is a serious missing ingredient for efficient and harmonious living in our society.* As people individually realize this, they'll be onto one of the highest intuitive breakthroughs ever on the planet.

Most people are only vaguely aware of their intuition. They mechanically seek outside answers for problems that develop within, rather than accessing the capabilities of their own *heart computer*. The heart is similar to a mainframe computer and has unexplored potentials of power and high-speed efficiency.

The human system was designed for efficient operation and the capacity for self-empowerment. View your heart as your center of control (mainframe) and your head (mind) as a sub-terminal used to help manifest the intuitive directives from the heart. The mind was designed as a helper, not as a leader. As this is understood, we will be halfway to victory in the stress war.

We, at the Intui-Tech center (a division of the Institute of HeartMath), have proven the intuition/heart connection to ourselves over the last several years as a result of searching for a self-responsible process of energy management. Please reserve your opinions of the heart/intuition theory until you have sincerely tried it, or you may be denying yourself a chance to learn an effective process for managing your stress.

True self-management will be a featured aspect of the next level of human intelligence—which is already expanding fast. It will be the "in thing" to pursue in the coming years. The next practical step in humanity's advancement will be to actually *live* our beliefs and "walk our talk," rather than turning others off with aggressive information that hasn't first been soundly proven in one's own backyard. People are looking for proof in action. They've heard all the self-righteous prescriptions for peace and are listening less.

In the future, only *living testimonies* of any peace mission will be effectively received by people en masse. Emotional (fear-based) conversions into any program have had their time. Now heart intelligence will have its time in creating an effective prescription for efficiency and peace in human relationships. It's time for individual mental and emotional management to be taken more seriously by all. This type of management would be evidence of higher intuition manifesting through human consciousness.

If you were told that you could wish for an intuitive manifestation of your choice, what would be your most efficient wish to manifest?

For some it would be the key to financial success; some would want to make a medical breakthrough; some would want to bring balance back into the ecology, etc., etc. These ideas would deserve special merit and would facilitate the planet. However, if you wanted to make a breakthrough that would address a critical need of humanity: You might consider first manifesting an efficient system that would facilitate people in *managing their own energies*. This facilitation would spawn more solutions for all the human and ecological ailments.

A self-responsible method of energy management will facilitate business, medicine, science, politics, social affairs, religion, economics—you name it. Intuitional innovation is much needed in all of these *isolated* areas. Still, new breakthroughs in these areas will only provide patchwork solutions for the whole, until we apply management to relationship and communication problems as well. As people realize the efficiency in *care* and *cooperation*, this will magnetize techno-biological advancement according to the need of the "now." First things first.

A Dimensional Shift in Time Management

The popular time management programs are evolving processes. They ultimately lead to self-management in their highest unfoldment. True self-management is actually a *dimensional shift in intelligence* compared to time management as it's understood today. As you achieve self-management, then managing time becomes an automatic process. This doesn't mean that you discard all your tools for time organization. It means that you are no longer boxed-in by them.

People who diligently practice time management programs often feel like they've become trapped by time rather than truly managing it. This happens when the head gets so involved in the procedures that it stifles the intuitive link to the heart. If you over-focus on managing time, you can short-circuit your possibilities for the next level—intuitive time management.

Quantum intelligence unfolds through the heart via intuition. As you learn how to activate this process, your relationship to time dramatically shifts into another level of freedom and creative innovation. Time management disciplines are valuable, like training wheels on a bike. They can guide you into the awareness of a more direct intuitive management that works at high speed. Intuitive management automatically accesses what action or direction would be the most effective in a moment of time measurement—an hour, day, week, month, etc.

The mind without heart can lose time-effectiveness by limiting itself to analytical and deductive reasoning processes. The mind is a wonderful gift, but there's a new dimension of intelligence to be unraveled as people look deeper into simplicity. To some, the heart sounds too simple to explore, and doesn't seem to offer the same intrigue as brain/mind research. But hidden within the simplicity of the heart lies a new doorway to understanding the mind and brain.

Your heart intuition has the capacity to engage your mind in producing subtle electrical frequencies which bring balance to the left and right hemispheres of the brain*. These encoded electrical patterns regulate the brain chemistry to increase the efficiency, integrity, and effectiveness of the brain and its functions. The balance of the two brain hemispheres creates one unified electrical signal. This signal then integrates with the heart and mind frequencies creating a triangulation of electrical resonance. As these three frequencies build in resonance, they form an energy field of intelligence that for all practical purposes translates into a third brain (which is electrical in nature, not physical). This third brain is designed to transmit and receive quantum intelligence and to differentiate it down through your physical brain network for practical use in day-to-day life. As the electrical triplicity between the heart, mind and brain builds into a standing wave of resonance, it creates a unified field of energy within the individual human mind that widens your perception. This electrical integration progressively activates the unused percentage of brain potentials that science acknowledges is dormant. Who would dare to believe that this can be achieved by learning how to follow your heart intuition and become your true self? Probably not science—yet.

The electrical third brain sounds like unsubstantiated theory, but so did acupuncture or the healing effects of prayer. The fact that acupuncture, prayer and other healing methods have worked on so many people is pressuring scientists to discover why, so that they can render their authoritative blessings and permission to believe in their effectiveness. A recent rigidly controlled scientific study by cardiologist Randolph Byrd, has shown that prayer *is*

---

*In his book *Vibrational Medicine*, (Bear & Company, © 1988) Richard Gerber, M.D., describes scientific researcher Bentov's discoveries on heart-brain resonance.

effective in healing. Even hard-boiled skeptics agree on the significance of Byrd's findings. In an article on the study by Dr. Larry Dossey, he quotes Dr. William Nolan, an author who had written a book debunking faith healing. Dr. Nolan now acknowledges, "It sounds like this study will stand up to scrutiny…. If it works, it works." You can be reaping the rewards of following heart intuition long before science is able to verify why it works.

What does this have to do with day-to-day time management? A lot. Following the heart is like using a master time management computer. It empowers your mind and brain to give you access to another dimension of time management. Managing time is not necessarily the same as being productive within a time span. It's similar, but there's a qualitative difference. Time management is about *planning*. Heart management is about *being*. In the state of *being*, planning becomes more of an intuitive flow, allowing you to make more effective choices regarding your use of time. Balancing the brain hemispheres with the heart activates both its creative and linear functions, creating a joint venture of efficiency and effectiveness.

Some people are highly creative but need to balance their creativity with left-brain practicality. Others are practical, linear-thinking types, but don't connect as much with their right-brain creative side. Once creative innovation is added to linear time management, you tremendously increase your effectiveness within the time value of the moment. The heart is the balance point within the ingenious blueprint of the human system and the emancipator of the clutches of time. Heart intelligence uses time for true effectiveness rather than a cage to live within.

Without heart intelligence, the mind tends to get so involved in the pieces of the puzzle that it can lose sight of the bigger picture. While the mind is well-equipped to orchestrate linear time management programs, *the overview of intuitive intelligence is required to orchestrate the mind*. Heart intuition is designed to manage the mind. It's also designed to put first things first, especially knowing what *is* first—what your true goals are. Heart intuition illuminates the mind with high speed choices that are aligned with your deeper values and intended purpose. When you manage the mind from the heart, you have more focused energy for carrying out your real priorities. It's worth the practice of listening more to your heart to develop that power to clarify and carry out your real priorities.

If you practice time management programs, then you know the importance of writing down your true values and the purpose you want to accomplish. Write down your priorities, but attempt to do it from the heart level and not just from the head. The heart will reveal what you're truly looking to achieve, while the head will tend to reach for the sky before building a bottom line foundation. It's okay to shoot for the sky, but go a step at a time and build solidly so that a gust of wind doesn't wipe out your whole intention. As you re-read your purpose statement, *sincerely feeling it in the heart*, you send strong electrical frequencies to the subconscious which then deeply imprints the conscious mind with your intentions. This creates *focused* power to manifest your vision of the bigger picture and not get sidetracked by the pieces of the puzzle.

My first priority is to arrange time to allow for sincere interactions with people. Building deeper relationships with people is valuable in anyone's bigger picture plan. It creates bonding and nurturing which empowers true quality experiences at work or at home. The bonus is this: when you put your deeper values first, the rest of your priorities and "to-do" lists seem to automatically re-arrange and fall in place with quantum effectiveness. It sounds simple but as I said earlier, simplicity is where the real smarts are hidden.

Subtle electrical activity activates your brain, so what activates your heart? Practice loving more and being more sincere with all people. That's the first step. Then practice managing your head from your heart and creating a joint venture between the two. This creates the electrical interaction which awakens the heart potentials to empower quantum intelligence. Listen more deeply to the quiet wisdom of your heart feelings for the most effective guidance throughout the day. This will take you past the present understanding of time management and into the capacity to effectively and efficiently arrange time as you see fit.

Love: Its Link to Intuitive Development

By learning to love more, you engage a higher frequency range of your heart's qualities, quickening your intuitive connection. Einstein, Gandhi, Schweitzer and other creative humanitarians had an obvious *care* for the whole.

A greater *understanding and practice* of love and care will usher in the highest demonstration of intuitive unfoldment yet on the planet. The inner voice is your radio frequency connection between heart intelligence and brain/mind consciousness. As this radio signal from heart intuition enters your physical brain, you become conscious of it. Then you have to actualize what you perceive if it's to be of value to yourself and others. Acting on those signals increases the amplitude and clarity of the intuitive transmissions within your system. Development is progressive, just like the process of learning how to run. After you start crawling, you learn to walk, and soon you're off and running. Simply said, the inner voice communicates to you through "feelings" that get clearer as you practice deeper listening. Don't give up after the first day of practice—you didn't when learning how to walk and run.

Learning how to separate your heart directives from your mental and emotional impulses is a good place to start intuitive education and self-management. Realize—"Your heart knows best." Heart intuition is there for the taking, yet it has been there the whole time. With sincere efforts, you can quickly develop a rapport with your heart feelings.

As more heart energy (love) is expressed through your nature, it changes the quality of your hormonal output, and with *regenerative* results. The way you perceive and experience stress is regulated by hormonal changes and mixtures in the glandular system. Your heart intelligence is your most dependable pharmacist. As you learn to love, you create internal prescriptions for a "high" that lasts.

As science understands that "love" is an intelligence unto itself, then researchers will more objectively respect its wide range of potentials. It's hard to scientifically investigate love, due to its present restrictive definitions and subjective associations (mushy, sentimental, romantic, poetic, religious, etc.). However, it can be done. The results will revolutionize our approach to all the physical and social sciences. Physics has already proven that once two particles touch, there's a connection between them that goes beyond space and time.

Love puts out a range of frequencies that can renew the quality of life on any level of your beingness, whether physical, emotional, mental or spiritual. Scientists are already beginning to test the effects of love in relationship to healing. Wait until they can *regulate* its tonic and healing effects on the mental and emotional nature. When science understands the frequencies of love, then scientific bulletins will read like a quote from Confucius— *"Science says: Love is the most efficient way."* Just a little humor, but time will find it to be truth in essence.

Scientists are already familiar with the mind/brain connection. Yet, in the relatively near future, the heart/emotions/mind/brain connection will be verified. Here at the Intui-Tech center, we are in the process of conducting new research to approach its scientific validation. An intention of Intui-Technology is to understand heart power on all levels and translate that understanding into a user-friendly system of self-empowerment for ordinary people—the biggest group of all.

An Intui-technique

Intui-Technology starts with becoming more consciously sensitive to your inner structure—your mental, emotional and intuitive natures. These aspects operate within you automatically, but there is an advantage if you can isolate them objectively. A technique for this is what we call *Freeze-Frame*.

Freeze-Frame means taking the time to stop and be still inside for a few minutes. You can do it any time, but it is especially useful when you feel overloaded or emotionally cloudy. When people are distressed, you often hear them say, "I've got to stop for a moment and get a hold of myself." That is an attempt at Freeze-Framing but often it doesn't work unless done from the heart.

When you Freeze-Frame, first attune to your heart, then make a gentle effort to still your emotions and quiet your racing mind. It's like turning an inner radio dial. You switch your focus of attention to a heart frequency—love, compassion, care, patience, appreciation, etc. Feel compassion for yourself or send thoughts of love or appreciation to someone. Doing this changes the quality of your energy and activates your heart power, making it easier to quiet the inner noise and static. Heart attunement often brings clear, unclouded perspectives that result in practical solutions. (This comes from your heart intelligence—it's a feeling of knowingness.)

Freeze-Frame is not only useful for solving problems. It's also good for creative inspiration. Freeze-Framing is not meditation or a mystical practice. It's just a deliberate inner stillness so that the dust from the mind and the emotions can settle. Then it's easier to see a different reality without distortion.

Freeze-Framing works especially well for anxiety. It gives your mind the equivalent of a back massage. When the mind is slowed down, then the heart intuition can more easily manifest into your conscious awareness. That starts to eliminate fears, anxieties, anger and the "poor me's" from your catalog of attitudes.

For example, if you're responsible for a new employee who

makes a large error, you can feel a reaction of anger arise; but if you Freeze-Frame and activate heart energy it balances your perspective. You may remember he's having a problem with his marriage as well as learning the new job. By activating your heart potential, you gain intuitive discrimination on how to best respond. You still take care of business, but with sensitivity and balance.

Practice Freeze-Framing and becoming more sensitive to your inner heart feelings. You will soon gain clarity on what is the heart and what is the head. Believe me, it's a worthy investment of your time and attention. Remember, having a good head on your shoulders is practical, but the head serves best as a right-hand helper to the heart. Intuitional manifestation is a joint venture between the heart and the head.

It's your heart-powered actions that give strength and completion to your intentions. That's why in sports people say "play from the heart," and kids are told to "tell the truth from the heart." Humanity is full of adages and references to the power and strength of the heart. "My heart didn't feel right about it." "His work is from the heart." "Let's get to the heart of the matter." I could go on.

Simplify it all by learning to "live from the heart," staying self-empowered and energy-efficient. Life is an economy game and managing from the heart yields to you more assets than deficits at the end of a day, week or year. It's worth intelligent consideration. Practice assessing things from a deeper point of truth within yourself.

Self-Esteem: A Spoke of Intuitional Unfoldment

If you looked at heart intuition as the hub of a wheel, then self-esteem would be one of the spokes. Big bucks are spent in the pursuit of: Personal Magnetism, Charisma, Sales Power, Self-Esteem. You can get all of the above in one package by learning to manage your life from heart intelligence.

To start with, self-esteem is much misunderstood, but many people share a common excitement about its potentials. The inability of people to agree on its definition and function creates cross-frequencies of understanding regarding the value of self-esteem within our society. If I may tamper with some of the current illusions, let me state that self-esteem is not the "panacea pie" that it often gets the credit for being. Relax, I'm not against self-esteem. I'm an advocate of the next level of intelligent understanding of the energy behind such a word.

The word "self-esteem" is an attempt to describe an electromagnetic energy that flows through the human system, creating self-confidence and "on-the-move" type feelings. Self-esteem is actually a description of certain isolated frequencies of *spirit* manifesting through one's system. If spirit were a pie, then self-esteem would be one of the slices—not the whole pie. Realize that high-achievers in business or school can win awards for self-esteem, yet their personal or social lives can be stressful and chaotic. Just because self-esteem can manifest in one isolated area of achievement doesn't mean that you have a high ratio of spirit manifesting in other areas of your life.

Spirit is like the iceberg and self-esteem is merely a tip of the possibilities of that spirit. You can't pigeonhole self-esteem and have it conform to idealistic extrapolations of what it should or should not be. Be careful of assigning a moral standard to self-esteem when it obviously can express itself differently in different people.

For example, amongst teenagers, a violent gang leader could have elevated levels of so-called self-esteem in isolated areas of his nature, but he obviously doesn't manifest the complete package. Some people would say that the gang leader, even though he has self-confidence, charisma and magnetism, doesn't have self-esteem at all because he's not acting in a way that's morally acceptable. How is he different from a powerful politician, peace activist, or salesman, all of whom may have self-esteem in isolated areas but the rest of their lives could be immoral by social standards?

The point I'm making is that you can't give self-esteem a moral code or definition before you understand the complex aspects of this energy. That's one of the first mistakes of many self-esteem enthusiasts. Face it, even a bank robber can have self-esteem in isolated areas—just like ministers, politicians, geniuses, or anyone. The whole concept of self-esteem will remain subject to controversy until people gain a more educated perspective of how spirit integrates into the human system.

Managing from the heart helps bring complete balance into your system, thereby allowing your *inner spirit* to increasingly manifest in your day-to-day world. This adds fun and fulfillment to your life, even if you've never heard the word self-esteem. Self-awakening through heart contact leads to the beneficial essence of what people call self-esteem, but in a *complete package* not just in a few isolated areas. Self-esteem is a *by-product* of being yourself. It's not a magical potion or a quick fix for life's problems by any means. However, as you experience more self-esteem (or more spirit flowing through your system) through heart management, it gets easier to dissipate the resistance of stress and find new areas of sparkle and achievement in your life.

Now that we've discussed some of the current confusion regarding self-esteem, let's look at some of its real potentials.

When love and self-worth permeate your system, they transform your fears and insecurities into what's called *self-esteem* (spirit integration). It's been acknowledged that self-esteem generates an ongoing confidence and is a powerful healing facilitator. It's an electromagnetic energy that, when generated, can transform the standing wave frequency patterns of many negative thoughts or attitudes. This gives your system more clarity so that you can make instant attitude adjustments when you're out of sync with yourself. As you maintain self-esteem, its frequency band helps keep non-efficient thoughts and attitudes in check—resulting in the discovery of your real self.

Self-esteem (an aspect of spirit) is simply an intelligent magnetism that generates balance and synchronicity between the heart/emotions/mind and brain. That's why people who are considered to have high levels of self-esteem often operate with more effectiveness, flexibility and adaptability. One spirit-generated attitude can start to rearrange and uplift the frequency patterns of a depressing day—just like turning a radio dial back to a good station. Self-negating attitudes, or poor self-image, create inner frequencies of distortion and static—like a radio stuck between stations.

Living from your *head* without *heart* balance will tend to unplug you from the energy tonic that self-esteem can provide. This causes your hormones to chemically prescribe you a dry and dismal *perspective* of life. Your perspective of life helps to determine the quality and fun you experience—or the "gloom" that saps your spirit. When self-esteem flows through you, it rounds off the *edges* of your interactions with day-to-day life—the mental and emotional edges—like insecurity, irritability, anxiety, feeling emotionally dry, etc. These feelings sap energy but offer nothing in return—except problems. Self-esteem energy, being an aspect of your spirit, connects you with your intuition and facilitates solutions to problems or helps you neutrally adapt to problems until a solution appears. As you learn to follow your heart and manifest your spirit more fully in your life, you develop self-esteem in its completeness, without the gaps.

If you can place yourself in the company of people who are infused with spirit, their energy gives you spark and facilitation— a confidence boost. Fortunately, the electricity of spirit is contagious. When this positive energy of well-beingness circulates through your system, people often refer to you as being "lit up." People lit with the flow of spirit can change a roomful of negative attitudes into a hopeful and cheerful environment even without verbal communication. Esteem instantly communicates itself to other people, especially to their feeling nature. Your heart is the connecting source of this regenerative energy and the wellspring of youthful vitality. As you learn to be yourself, this energy will flow more consistently.

You can only develop a more complete sense of esteem to the degree that you eliminate the fears and insecurities from your system. Sorry, you can't cheat your way "in" with high energy rallies and reciting positive thinking verses. Those are good and do facilitate, but your *heart-powered commitment* has to give life to your positive affirmations if you want to achieve self-empowerment.

Heart intuition can efficiently guide you through a step-by-step transformational process of *re-educating* your insecurities, fears and mind-sets. Remember, mind-sets are crystallized attitudes that hinder the expansion of intelligence; they keep you bound to insecurities and tunnel vision. With practice, you can transform mind-sets and insecurities into flexibility and peace with being yourself. It won't be the long journey that you might anticipate if you start now.

Each time you manage yourself from the heart, you increase the power of confidence which translates into more self-esteem— or more of your true spirit manifesting through your nature. As you become your true self and draw from your inner strength, your self-security and confidence multiply exponentially. Then the flow of your spirit is boosted to *the automatic pilot control level*. (That's when you don't have to work to manifest it. You *are* it.)

Whatever it takes to learn the *heart way*, it's well worth it many times over. It's not a new religion nor does it compete with religious practices. It's about "you and yourself"—a personal system that can create more efficiency in your day-to-day life. Check it out.

An Overlooked Relationship
The One With Yourself

The world news implies that the planetary relationship equilibrium is askew. How about yours? Have you, from a self-truth perspective, taken a recent look at your *relationships* —with people, places and things (i.e., family, friends, work, money, beliefs, issues)? Do you ever ponder the amount of energy loss or stress you experience each day, month or year because of on-running relationship distortions?

One disharmonious relationship with *anything* or *anybody* can generate an enormous *accumulation* of stress. If you could record your *stress deficit* for one year—stress that was accumulated from disharmony in relationships—you would realize why you sometimes feel less vitality and spark than you should or why you don't enjoy life the way you used to. Not everyone experiences this, but many do. Just as positive energy creates assets in return—so does disharmony create deficits in return. Energy goes out and comes back (that's physics).

One of the biggest causes of disharmony and energy deficits is the tendency to judge. I'm not referring to the judgments passed in the judicial system. I'm talking about the automatic judging of people, places or issues that subtly drains your system without your even knowing what happened. The *head* forms these judgments when it is out of phase with the *heart*. Let's take a deeper look.

Judgments

Have you ever noticed how it feels when someone judges you, and the stress that it can create if you let it? Yet it's so mechanical and natural for people to judge each other without even thinking twice. Well, it's really *not* natural to judge people. *Nature* doesn't judge. It allows. Judging is the opposite of allowing people to *be*. Your true nature is to live and let live, while attending to your own turf. That's the most efficient thing you can do for yourself and for the people you would judge.

Many people cleverly dismiss their judgments as *assessments*. That approach isn't so clever if you realize almost everyone else does the same. Let's say your boss has made a decision which you think is unwise. Your head quickly assesses how you would do it differently. Then you assess him as lacking in intelligence and understanding. You mentally list his other faults and wonder how he made it to the top. You feel separate from him and keep your distance at the office. Without realizing it, your assessments have turned into judgments.

It's comfortable to pass judgments off as assessments until they are directed at *you*. Then you keenly realize that people's assessments of you are often judgments in disguise. In life, we need to make assessments and discernments, and use discrimination. These processes of evaluation facilitate when done from the *heart*. When done from the *head*, without care and latitude from the heart, these evaluations create separatism, condescension, self-righteousness and hurt. Until people learn to assess, discern and discriminate with the heart, these words will remain hiding places for outright judgments.

Habitual patterns of judging crystallize you into *"knowing what you know."* If you're too rigid in "knowing what you know," you put ceilings on your capacity to learn and experience. This can inhibit mental and emotional growth and fulfillment and eventually lead to disease.

The tendency to judge (or self-judge) is often caused by a lack of security in isolated areas within yourself. It's the bondage to fears, envies and insecurities that keeps humanity from enjoying the freedom of spirit and real quality in experience. As you learn to live from the truth in your heart, your feelings of security increase and your judgments decrease. Self-security replaces judgments with compassion. Compassion and understanding facilitate, while judgments debilitate and create stress. It's hard to beat compassion or care when *you* need them. It's also hard to beat off the effects of judgments or condescension towards **you** when you don't need them. Realize the importance of being sincere from the heart when you weigh out the actions of other people. That's what you would want for yourself, is it not?

In the example above, let's say you decided to make a heart assessment of your boss instead of just a head assessment. You attempt to still the head reactions and shift your focus of attention to the heart. You decide to sincerely feel compassion for him for a few moments. This gives the heart intuition a chance to show you a broader view of the situation. Even if you still perceive your boss's decision as unwise, you gain a wider perspective. You continue to send him compassion and understanding while listening to your heart intuition for what the best response would be.

There's an emotional starvation among people to be accepted, understood and not judged. This need won't be filled until people individually accept the responsibility to put out to others what they would want in return. As you learn to filter life through your heart, then mechanical head judgments will cease and be replaced by more compassion and care.

Self-judgments can dilute your system as fast as judging

other people. Practicing sincere compassion for your own growth process is a remedy for that. Realize that self-judgments and self-beating only make things worse. Don't just listen to my words; your heart will give you your own answer. You often hear people say, "I've got to quit judging myself because I know it's making matters worse." That's their heart coming through—the inner voice of wisdom.

If you're self-judging and being hard on yourself, just wake up one morning and affirm in your heart that you're going to **quit it.** Then, when you find yourself chewing on self-judgment during the day, practice REMEMBERING that you were going to **quit that**. As you use the power of your heart, you can, at times, gently release those thoughts and quit giving them energy to exist. Don't underestimate what you can do when you *sincerely* mean business about something. (Many people have even told themselves that.) Self-judgment is like a log in the path. It's a self-imposed block to your personal progress. It stifles the energy that could be supplying you with more happiness and fulfillment.

In observing yourself, notice when judgmental attitudes arise towards yourself, other people or issues. Then make efforts to replace these attitudes with *latitude*. By this, I mean cut yourself and others more slack. Realize that when you're judging someone, you've probably been there before or may be in that same situation next week. Try to at least take a *neutral* position. That creates balance in your own system and especially reduces stress.

In the beginning, it's hard to replace your judgments with compassion or care. But if you at least learn to neutralize judgmental attitudes, you'll save yourself much energy. With practice, you can learn to send out the quality of thoughts and feelings you would want in return. Constant judging from the head keeps you from experiencing the real connection in relationships and events in life. Often you miss the enjoyment of another person's true essence because of pre-set judgments about their character or some quirk.

There are possibly people who have crossed your path in life who could have (because of their nature) become your best friends. You may never have gotten to know them because of conditioned judgmental attitudes such as: "He works for PEPSI," when you work for COCA-COLA; "they eat meat," when you're a vegetarian; "he's a truck driver," but you're an executive; "she's pro-choice," and you're not. These are only a few examples of pre-set judgmental attitudes that hold people back from deeper communication and potential fun in relationships. I didn't even mention the separatism caused by religious differences or political issues. That would require a whole book.

It's natural to resonate more with certain types of people, but it's still important to be free from judgmental mind-sets so you don't limit your possibilities for richer relationships. You can free yourself from mind-sets and pre-judgments by the practice of relating to all people from the sincere heart. Then your heart intuition will allow you to experience the real essence in people— and not miss it because of judgments or pre-conditioned opinions.

Here's a fun hands-on exercise: As you are reading this book, try to at least neutralize any tendency to judge or get upset if I say things that rub you the wrong way. Doing this will help you remember the points that you do resonate with and can use. Use what you like and try not to over-react to what you don't. That's *allowing*. In this way, you're practicing heart discrimination rather than reactive head judgment. If you apply this exercise to other issues and other people as well, then you're demonstrating self-security and you're on your way to self-empowerment. (But, if you find yourself slipping into judgments while reading, no big deal. I realize the book deals with some sensitive and volatile issues. So, with understanding, I'll respect your differences of opinion.)

Now that we've discussed judgments, let's look at other energy deficits and some ideas on how to turn them into assets.

The Budget Sheet:
Mental and Emotional Energy Expenditures

Have you noticed how people look at a financial spread sheet and say: "We've got to tighten up," or "We're deep in the red this month," or "We broke even," or "We're in the black"? People are serious about monitoring their finances, but they don't take mental and emotional energy expenditures seriously.

You can create an imaginary budget sheet to see how your own mental and emotional assets and deficits stack up. The budget sheet concept can help you objectively realize why more people are not experiencing quality in life with health, peace and real fun. By the end of a year, lots of people have more energy deficits than assets on their mental and emotional budget sheets— especially in the area of relationships. It would probably cause global shock if people suddenly realized how much energy drain and deficit they experienced during a year because of *insecurities* and other problems within their relationships.

Try this:

1) Add up your distortions experienced in the past month or year—with people, work, traffic, social and personal issues, etc.

2) Then, remember the mental, emotional and physical stress resulting from those accumulated distortions. That's your deficits column. By deficit, I'm including those times when you were unhappy and frustrated because someone wasn't the way you wanted them to be, or caught up in overcare and drained by attachment, or resentful of someone's attributes or savvy, or hurt because of a lack of attention. (It goes on and on, creating serious energy drains.)

3) Now, add up your happy times—when you were loving and caring, or peaceful, or enjoying life, or when things seemed to go your way. These make up your assets column. Consider how your assets and deficits balance out. This gives you a chance to glimpse how much of your time spent is not quality time but could be, with

self-energy management.

I don't expect you to actually write down all your good and bad times throughout an entire year. Your own heart can give you feedback on the difference between your assets and deficits if you are sincere in wanting to know. Ask your true self-intuition for illumination concerning your inefficiencies in relationships. Assess if you are creating negative feedback loops that drain your life force daily. Are you complaining about the painful results of something that *you* are causing, by constantly setting yourself up to be hurt?

Even if you think you've had a good year, consider how much better it could have been if you'd managed your energies more efficiently and prevented the drain from those out-of-sync relationships. Many say they've had a good year, not because it was so good, but because they know it could have been worse—*considering*. Sure, that's thinking positive (sort of), but it's a spirit-wearied way to conclude that it was a good year. Each tough year can be made a better year by learning to adapt or make productive changes. Each good year can be made a great year—if you learn to follow your heart intuition and get the excess stress out of your face.

You'll recognize the advancement of planetary intelligence when people start to spend even one-tenth the time doing budget assessments on energy expenditures as they now spend on their *financial* budgets. Society's intelligence did increase in the last ten years as people started to become more conscious of their physical health. Many people began to realize that they could accumulate and maintain more physical energy by exercising and being conscious of their diets. That's important, but still, the physical is only one aspect to consider when you talk about energy management, self-maintenance and quality control. You can have perfect health and still be extremely unhappy and stressed because of emotional distortions over relationships, job loss, insecurities, etc.

You can't *see* the mind or emotions, but rest assured they are there and are "forces to be reckoned with." These two forces drag society around the block time and time again, year after year. Management and balance of these two aspects of your nature is laying the foundation for future peace and efficient communication between people.

People want an overnight cure for stress, but it's only they who can bring it about. As each one of us takes the steps towards self-responsibility, it helps others do the same. Almost everybody is waiting for someone else to do something, while complaining about stress and blaming it on other people or other issues.

Heart Intuition in Relationships: A Common Sense Strategy

Sometimes a person can't see *self-truth* because of insecurities or attachments to people and issues. Your securities are within you, waiting for a wake-up call. Your heart intuition can give you a clear perspective of what *drains* or *adds* energy to your system. The heart assessment just **is**. It's not blinded by insecurity, emotional colorations, mind-sets or attachments. The quality of relationships will upgrade once people practice more sincerity and deeper care for each other. This is not meant to be philosophical or sweet—it's common sense or *streetsense*. In the *old* intelligence, common sense was usually arrived at through the pain of repeated mistakes. In the *new* intelligence, heart intuition can direct you with common sense and save you from the unnecessary pain of non-efficient energy expenditures.

As I indicated earlier, intuition is like knowing something without having to go through the grind to get it. Like others, I have attended many popular seminars on intuition. They were informative, yet I learned more about intuition in a short period of time by listening to my heart than I ever learned in any seminar or book. The first step was realizing that the heart *was* a convenient voice for my intuition. I had often wondered why everybody talked about the "still small voice." I never stopped to think it was because that "voice" made sense. Each time I stilled the mind enough to listen to my heart feelings, I noticed that much less stress resulted from my choices and decisions. This led me to a deeper, more objective relationship with myself that had been missing.

I clearly saw that my mind, without heart management, often led me into business and relationship hassles. As I practiced seeing issues from the heart perspective, relationships became smoother. Daily decision-making took on a new clarity, creating more confidence in my choices. Like many people, I needed that. Heart intelligence is a source of free discrimination. Developing heart listening is a process that continually refines your discrimination. I can still make non-efficient choices, but it's easier to detect the energy drains and make corrections. As you strengthen the connection with your intuition, you develop quick, clear feedback when your decisions are out of phase with what's best for you.

I've talked a lot about intuition, though this chapter is on relationships. Here's why. It's the lack of intuitive development that causes relationship-gridlocks on the planet. Divorce statistics wouldn't be as high if intuition were flourishing. To start with, as you develop intuition it gets easier to discriminate compatibility. Many people are attracted to each other on physical or sexual levels and off to the altar they go. In the novelty of their sexual escapades, they fool each other (and themselves) into thinking they are also mentally and emotionally compatible, and even soul mates—or something.

Passion from sex novelty creates hormonal intoxication that blinds intuitive discrimination concerning relationship compatibility. Next comes marriage, then comes baby, then comes divorce and a child strewn through the middle of it. This scenario will continue until the intuition is more developed on the planet. I use the analogy of sexual delusion because many younger people, especially, fall blindly into that trap. Sure, everyone has heard all this before, but it's obvious they haven't *really* heard it at a deep level. You can hear it from the *head* level and fall into the same trap tomorrow. When you hear something from the *heart,* then you draw more strength to start acting on the wisdom of it.

Improving Self-Relationship

Many people separate or get divorced when they really are (or were) compatible. Because of a lack of individual management, their compatibility didn't get a chance to gel. So, if you really want to help a troubled relationship, assess *yourself* at a deeper heart level. As you re-balance your own self through heart management, you begin to see others from a different perspective and understand them through different feelings. If people do that, they'll have a good chance of saving a relationship or at least maturely separating.

Lack of self-maturity is the leading cause of relationship problems. Becoming your true self progressively develops that maturity. Start by performing spring cleaning on your own inner junk, while at the same time becoming more sensitive to the other person's needs. Watch for self-centeredness. It clogs the pipes of your sensitivity to others. It's a mechanical habit of the mind that causes people to think it's others who always need to change. You can drain yourself trying to arrange people to suit your mental and emotional needs. Rearranging your own attitudes puts you on the fast track to self-security and peace.

Build a heart-secure relationship with *yourself,* so you can enjoy relationships with others without crossing the line into over-dependency. Remember, over-dependency is an invitation for pain. Sure, people often have to depend on each other to help them through situations. That's a shared warmth in life. However, when you cross the line into over-dependency on mental and emotional levels, you lose the ability to connect with your own self-supporting inner strength. I'm not denying the importance of supportive intimacy, I'm just hinting at keeping a mature, balanced perspective. Trust more in your heart—it's the real security behind the scenes in life.

I've experienced several relationship perplexities in the past. It was worth the frustration just to realize that I had to get my own act together before I could expect harmony with someone else. I eventually learned balance and respect—but through *changing myself,* not others.

If you want to add some taxing miles to the "ol' bod," then get involved in a relationship before you're *heart smart* and matured yourself. Life will smarten you right up as it's doing to millions of people daily. Stress is impersonal, yet it breeds profusely in the environment of self-ignorance. Though it's innocent ignorance, it keeps people on the treadmill until their heart intelligence illuminates the way out.

As consciousness matures, people will realize that they have a *self-stress release system* on the inside. Money and education don't guarantee relief from stress. You could say, "Money and education sure do help!" For each one who says that, I can produce two who are rich, well-educated, stressed and depressed. Sure, money and education help, but so can rain, sunshine and toilet paper. The rich and poor alike will evolve into the understanding that stress dissipation is about developing the higher adapting process within one's own self.

Your heart intelligence can help you get off the head merry-go-round of constantly thinking about and amplifying your problems. It would startle most people to have a computer readout weekly, showing the amount of time they spent thinking and emoting over their problems. Then, if you had another computer readout showing the amount of negative hormones released into the body as a result of those thinking habits, you soon would want to make some mental and emotional adjustments. Computers can't generate all that data yet, so you don't have to face the facts. Yet, the facts of stress will find you—anyhow. The stress deficit accrues, whether or not you are conscious of it.

I realize it's hard not to churn your problems and I'm not idealistically saying you shouldn't. Still, you can learn to manage your non-efficient thinking and emotions. Just learn to be as conscious of your *mental and emotional energy expenditures and returns* as you are conscious of your *dollar* expenditures and returns. Remember the mental and emotional budget sheet. If you *halfway* play with this concept, it can give you a new perspective on energy economy.

Getting Beyond Dollar Hypnosis

Stress will cause people to re-evaluate their *value systems* in this decade. "Lord Dollar" will one day be dethroned and no longer revered as the king of security. The dollar will still be appreciated, but with balance.

Well, you could say that you're not controlled by money. But it would depress most people to realize just how much of their life is designed around the security of money versus that which is fun and fulfilling for them. Whether people think they're seduced by money or not, the rich and poor alike are victimized by its security trappings. The twist is that people want money to secure more conveniences and enjoyment, or for basic survival. Yet, they often sacrifice their true peace and happiness in their ambitious pursuit of more money. Money can add to security but can't be depended upon for inner balance and happiness. Heart intelligence can facilitate the balance of this non-efficient social quagmire.

Each day thousands of people take jobs they don't like, often leaving jobs they enjoyed, just because the pay is a few dollars more. If you are attracted to the extra dollars in a new job, be sure to consider the extra stress that is often caused in many job transitions. Use your heart to decide these things—not money infatuation. The mental and emotional stress caused by "dollar-hypnosis" adds to society's relationship failures and distortions, especially the relationship between people and themselves.

Because of the years of reverence that people innocently, yet ignorantly, have invested in "$Lord dollar$," society stays mesmerized and casually seduced from the realization of life's true value system. The statistics would be appalling if you realized the number of relationships and families that were destroyed because of unfulfilling job changes made for just a few more bucks and some vanity credits.

[A *vanity credit* is what you get when you cram yourself into another job position with a bigger title and name plate, even though it causes you much more stress than your previous employment. You may get a temporary vanity boost, but is it really worth the extra stress just for "name's sake?" Some changes are for the better and we all know that. But weigh out the stress involved. Your heart is wiser than your head when making these types of decisions. It takes a blending of the two to arrive at the most fulfilling choices when considering major transitions.]

Many family and personal relationships get stretched beyond repair because of "title climbing," "getting ahead" and "ambition-hypnosis." Unbalanced ambition is a *social predator* that's draining the heart out of business, government, family, children and individuals. Sure, ambition has its attributes. However, ambition without heart discrimination breeds self-centeredness and tunnel vision—resulting in insensitivity to people and losing sight of the things that matter. In the future, decisions will be made favoring family, mental and emotional health, and personal peace—rather than decisions that are hypnotically manipulated by *ambition* and *money*. This will help to introduce a new era of efficiency and integrity into the human system.

As you learn to make heart-based decisions, you will find balance in what's best for the *whole* and not just the part. Ask your heart, "Is what I'm attempting to do what I *really* want? Is it truly efficient? Is it the best for all concerned?" Your heart intuition knows what would make you feel the best after all is said and done. It's *sincere* asking that gives you a deeper feeling of inner knowing.

If you just listen to your head, you'll often find yourself jumping on someone else's "bandwagon" and attempting things that are not appropriate for your particular mental, emotional or physical makeup. What's right for *one* is not always right for *another*. Your heart knows the difference.

Sometimes life is looking out for you when it doesn't give you what you want exactly when you want it. Often, you come to realize that what you thought you wanted wouldn't have been the best after all. It's fun to make changes in life, but by doing it from the heart perspective you become more aware of what you are getting into.

There are many different aspects of relationship maladies I could mention, but the relationship with *yourself* is the vital issue. If you attempt to balance your own energy system, you'll see magic in your relationships with other people and the world.

Don't depend on people, places or things for your peace. That's just *conditional* peace and isn't necessarily dependable, even if you get it. The dream for an "over-the-counter-peace" is out the window and it's you who finally has to make your own peace from the inside out. Freeze-Frame the mind chatter, listen to your heart feelings, and develop your intuition. This will build *inner security* and advance you in the real peace-making process. Take the first step. The next step will show itself along the way—especially if you don't hold onto anxieties about the journey.

The Family Concept
The Hub of Efficiency

I could give you updated trend statistics to prove that the "Family Concept" is making its way back into mainstream consciousness. However, giving statistics is not the nature of this book; its intention is to stimulate the statistics of your *own* energy expenditures. This leads to self-empowerment. Facts and references are helpful, especially if you're talking about diet, disease, economics, etc. Yet, when used as a substitute for plain talk about sensitive issues, they often stifle intuitive assessment. Trends prove that what are *today's facts and statistics* won't necessarily be *tomorrow's truths*.

If you scan the TV occasionally or glance at a few magazines, you will realize that *family* ambience is on its way **in**. In the future, workplaces, political issues, social systems, etc., will have to adjust themselves around this unfolding actuality. It's a time for investing in *inner security and happiness*. So, the new trend will be the so-called "family trend," but let me add: The family concept is not really a trend, it just **is**—waiting for people to re-remember it.

The *family concept* is like a tree trunk; *trends* are like the limbs of a tree which set out to explore their own growth and creativity, while wisely connecting back to the trunk for strength and security. As people get lost in the glamour and stimulation of trends, they cut themselves off from the trunk of the family concept. The *head* is the part of you that explores stimulation and potential, yet often forgets its connection to the *heart,* which is the *family caretaker*—the trunk of your real security.

The family frequency bands are the feelings and intuition contained within your heart. They give you access to love, care, security, nurturing, bonding, family interaction, relationship frequencies, and more. As head frequencies of ambition and fast-lane living began to dominate society, the value system of the family unit became distorted and weakened. As people ambitiously pursued the glitter of high-tech and tempting opportunism, the *family concept* was reduced to a mere pilot light rather than a fire to warm by.

Many families today are united in namesake but are missing the *sensitivities* and *care* that foster family fulfillment. Basic survival is getting tougher and requiring much more energy—both parents needing to work, children being raised at day care, the cost of living increasing, unemployment rising—these are all survival issues with no efficient solutions being offered. The accumulated stress has to be dealt with—and soon. For social intelligence to progress, we will first have to drop back a few notches and fill in the unattended holes. Yes, back to basics—the *family concept*. (The social heart.)

The caring in business, the caring in politics, the caring in education, the caring about the ecology, the *caring* in all major people departments has taken a beating like an un-recouped stock market crash. When *care* is revitalized in the social system, the "stock market of life" will flourish. If *CARE* were a stock being offered on the market, it would be a wise commodity to invest in at this time on the planet. Care will soon be on the rise because everything else has been tried. As people connect more sensitively with their family frequencies, you will see the *textures* of care increase in all people interactions. It won't happen overnight, and people problems stand to get worse before they get better. But there is a way out.

Care is one of our most effective outgoing energy expenditures—it is *love* in the active modality. As people self-empower, through following their hearts' directives, they will naturally experience a deeper care for all people and for the Earth. *This deeper, more sincere, family-type-caring-for-people is the missing ingredient in the recipe for harmonious living. It's a powerful solvent for the compounded stress perplexity that encumbers the planet and its people.*

You've often heard the phrase: "Give peace a chance." Unfortunately, *peace* won't get a chance until *care* has had its chance. Wishful slogans and philosophies have had their time. Now it's time for action—*self-initiated* action to reactivate the care frequencies within individuals. Managing life through your heart's perspective re-kindles the family spirit. This creates more buoyancy and quality feelings in your life's adventure.

Understand that I'm not glorifying the "family concept" just because it has a sweet and sentimental aura. I'm talking about a practical business understanding of family for developing self-empowerment and the capacity to manage your own stress! I can appreciate the sentiment that goes with the word *family*; but there is a lot more to be understood about family than just biological relationships. I'm especially talking about bringing the family concept into business and all social issues—in the name of psychological and business integrity. Businesses strive for efficiency but fall short in "warmth" when the family frequencies are not considered in their structures and plans. *Heart efficiency has warmth, integrity and effectiveness within its meaning.* Mind efficiency (without heart integration) can be dry and mechanical. The mind alone is often ineffective in manifesting the higher values and purposes of business, of family or personal life.

Family is determined by the degree of heart resonance you feel with someone. This explains how you sometimes have a deep connection with certain friends or co-workers, similar to the one you have with family at home. In many cases, people feel more resonance with friends (because of other interests) than they do with their own families. As people become heart-conscious, they will experience family resonance with more and more people. This doesn't take away from the special feeling you have with your hub family or your closest friends. Extended family resonance has the power to stimulate a tonic and healing effect among individuals and society. Heart-generated interactions release positive hormones into your body that act as protective soldiers to your immune system.

Your heart resonance increases when your communication is more *sincere* with all people in business, social and personal matters. It's about learning how to treat people the way **you** want to be treated yourself. I'm not trying to sound biblical—this is a statement of common sense.

Many people think that if they expand their *care* past a small circle, they will be taken advantage of, hurt, used, etc., etc. However, as you really learn to care more and treat people with more respect, you build *self-security* within yourself—not weakness and vulnerability.

More and more, people are looking for proven-out systems that facilitate deeper caring without the *fear* of being hurt. Systems that facilitate self-empowerment through personal energy management will be in demand. People will look for systems that promote self-security *without* having to depend on people, places or things for personal peace. The need for a balanced system of communication will become more obvious than ever. Utilizing your own personal heart smarts is a good place to start efficient communication. Use the genie in your own lamp, the voice of your heart intuition.

Increasingly, you will see society demanding more *care*: from businesses, family, friends, government. This is happening already and eventually it will become a social standard. Again, I offer you a stock market tip: *Real Care* is a good "now" investment for future dividends in peace, adventure and abundance.

One strong indication of the return to the family concept is the increasing number of men who are playing an active and sensitive role in parenting. Men have both male and female energies within them and so do women. Many men are learning to bring the female aspects of their nature into balance with their male energies. This will increase their overall sensitivity and capacity to understand women. Many women are going through a similar process but with the emphasis on balancing the male side of their nature with their feminine side.

Women have become more active and capable in male-associated activities over the past years—in business, sports, military, etc., etc. This is because they are responding to an innate impulse to bring the male aspects of their nature into balance. As women balance these two natures, they contact more of the potential security within their own selves. However, it's important for women not to over-develop the male side while finding balance, or they can lose touch with their heart and their nurturing side.

Nurturing

When men and women stop nurturing each other in relationships, life gets dry, problems breed. A lack of nurturing is like having a vitamin deficiency in your mental and emotional nature. It's a serious *necessity* and often goes unattended.

Nurturing starts as *care* reaches heightened sensitivity. As people become truly cared for, they have a better chance of developing their self-security in life's maturing process. Women have a more natural tendency towards nurturing because of child-birthing capabilities which enable them to generate the securities demanded by a new life form. Single-parent men usually proceed quickly in the balancing of their male and female aspects. This is because single parenting demands feminine frequencies of conscious care and acute sensitivities for protection.

Men have within them tremendous *nurturing* frequencies. With practice, these energies can be brought from the subconscious and create a more enriched relationship to all life. Don't be someone who thinks that nurturing is putting food on the table and a roof over the family's head. That's *providing*, not *nurturing*. Many divorces have taken place because of this one misunderstanding. It's nice to provide but it's a good place to hide—from the understanding of nurturing. Food on the table can feed your face but nurturing kindles the spirit of a person's existence. Communication at the essence level is where real strength is exchanged in relationships.

If you are interested in learning to enhance your nurturing aspects, then practice caring for whomever you are with at a deeper and more sensitive level. Nurturing starts with a sensitive *caring* and an appreciation of someone more deeply than just at the personality level of communication. Sometimes caring and appreciation are active, sometimes passive, but potent either way.

It takes a little effort and courage to activate the nurturing process. It gets easier as you practice because it adds *quality* to your experiences and de-stresses your system. If your relationships with other people are quality ones, then the rest of life's problems are easier to deal with—no matter what. When your relationship life is troubled, then the quality of life devaluates at high speed—turning your day-to-day environment into a lackluster existence.

The development of a deeper "hearing ability" helps to awaken your nurturing capabilities. Deeper listening will do much to eliminate what men call "nagging." Nagging is often a cry in despair to be understood. After a year or so of not being heard or understood, nagging evolves into (so-called) bitching. Finally, how could it not. This will dissipate tremendously as men develop their nurturing side.

Like many men, I expected women in my life to be sensitive to my needs, since I thought I was sensitive to theirs. Yet, they would tell me they often felt unheard and would accuse me of not caring. After several stress-producing relationships, I started sincerely searching for answers and realized that I was the one who needed refining.

One of the most helpful things I discovered was that I needed to develop a deeper hearing ability. When dealing with women, I tended to know all the answers before they even stopped talking. This doesn't work. It creates out-of-phase communication. The less aggressive person usually ends up misunderstood or stifled in these situations. By listening more sincerely, my sensitivity increased. That brought my nurturing side into balance with my assertive male nature. Sincere listening and care can nurture male/female communication and understanding into a new level of awareness.

As men and women become more balanced within themselves, they will naturally develop the understanding and sensitivity that they demand or expect. Then, they'll be able to give children the understanding and nurturing needed for future self-security.

Self-Security in Children

Many single-parent women fear that their children won't get enough male influence in their growth and development. Single-parent men face this question in reverse. The answer can depend on how balanced your own male/female nature is as an individual. If you are unbalanced in your male or female nature, it often affects your children's personality development, creating patterns of insecurity that plague them into adulthood. (Children are resilient, so this isn't always the case.) Here are some home remedies to help prevent this.

A most efficient approach is to teach children to follow their hearts at a young age. They are more responsive to heart understanding than you may think, especially if you are attempting to practice it yourself. The earlier that children learn to check things out with their heart feelings, the more they stay balanced as they grow and create inner security along the way. Building a foundation of inner security and personal esteem early on is important, because schools tend to rob children of these qualities as they progress through the educational system. This is due primarily to the mandate of a head-based curriculum and overcrowded classrooms where children's unique differences are often not addressed.

With one parent, two parents or none, children are much more likely to come out balanced and happier if they are taught a system of self-security. Through innocent ignorance, a high ratio of parents teach their children to depend on them for emotional security until the time they leave home to become adults. That seems sweet but is an inferior way to package a kid to face life out in the world. This is one of the reasons why teens have so many emotional distortions—*a lack of self-security training*. Without learning self-security, children have difficulty becoming who they really are.

Self-security training should be high on the list of what's important in child-rearing. Outer security is important for children, but it's inner security (or the lack of it) that especially affects the rest of their lives. If children learn heart management at an early age, they'll be secure and well-adjusted to face adulthood. Observe and see if you are causing your children to depend on you too much for their inner security. You can save yourself much emotional wear and tear in the future by monitoring this process and teaching them how to be secure within themselves.

Another home remedy: Practice heart management systematically day-to-day yourself. This will balance your inner male and female energies and encourage a balance in your children. It's a most important gift to them.

Here's a game to help children develop an understanding of the difference between their reactive head thoughts and their intuitive voice from the heart.

Let a child know when s/he is not in the heart. For example, tell a child, "You're pouting (whining, screaming, having a temper tantrum, not listening, etc.) and that's your head voice, not your real heart voice. So, let's take a moment to *Freeze-Frame*. Let's *stop*, *relax* and *listen*." (In the beginning it takes a little coaching.)

Let children know that *stop* means to try to be still inside. (Children can understand that better than you may think—with some help.) After they *stop*, tell them, "Now, in a *relaxed* way, we can *listen* to each other." (This will help children to express themselves without the emotional distortion. It de-stresses their system and teaches them clear communication.)

After you get children to *stop, relax* and *listen*, then say, "Now, you are in your heart. Now, from your heart feelings, tell me what you really want to say. Just talk slowly and clearly, like you're telling me a story about someone else. And I'll listen carefully, okay?" With a little practice, children will understand what you mean when you tell them, "You're out of your heart," or "Get back in your heart." (Often, they understand this more quickly than adults do. They haven't been programmed with all the mind-sets or mind tricks that people learn as they grow older. That's why adults often wish they were children again. Today, many people are trying to re-connect with their inner child. This is because they miss that spontaneous connection with the heart that a child has.)

As a child speaks from the heart, you often notice a voice change—a less edgy, softer, and more sincere voice. Remind children of that and help them to realize they talk differently when they're *not* in their hearts. As children learn to speak from the heart, you will experience an even more intelligent rapport. However, while communicating, if they start to slip back into whining and pouting, gently stop them and point out, "You're getting out of your heart again." Reaffirm to them, "Slow down and get back in your heart before you speak." Ask them, "Can't you hear the difference in your voice when you're speaking from your heart and when you're whining from the head?" With coaching, they will soon recognize that difference.

Tell them, "It's easier to fix the problem if you're in the heart." (If they're in the heart, then youngsters can understand and adapt more easily when things don't always go the way they want. Once children shift to their heart feelings, their problems tend to re-solve much faster.) After they get familiar with this game, you don't have to go through the whole process. You can just tell them, "Get back in your heart," and you'll often notice them arriving at their own stress-free solutions.

This simple technique gets children started in managing their energies from the heart. Once they learn this at home, it can carry over into other relationships at school and all other environments. It's a building block for self-responsibility. When children learn the knack for heart management, they build confidence, inner security and true esteem at an early age.

As you practice with them, it gets easier to identify the times when children are not connected in the heart. Soon you'll auto-matically know the difference. Remember, if you want this game to be effective, then be in your own heart while teaching children. This technique helps to create a deeper and lasting bond between parent and child because it's building a solid bottom-line for a true relationship. You'll especially learn a lot about your own heart directives in the process—that's the bonus point. Realize that it's easy for parents to see when children are out of the heart. But, after the kids learn the heart game, they're very quick to notice when parents are out of their hearts—and they'll let *you* know it! When sincerely helping children, life will always reward you with a deeper awareness of yourself. The heart games can help sustain, right into adulthood, the natural heart bonding that a parent and child have from birth through the first few years.

This is not really the book to elaborate on children's issues or games. However, my next book will be on how to teach young children to manage life from the heart. It will be a fun family workbook designed to help bridge the generation gaps that often occur in families. (My last book, *The How-To Book of Teen Self Discovery,** shows teenagers how they can learn to manage their lives from the heart. Written in language that they can relate to, it addresses many of the issues that teens and parents cope with day-to-day. When parents and teens read the book together, it facilitates a deeper bonding and understanding.)

To sum up, the safe bet for remedies involving family per- plexities is to become *heart-managed* yourself and teach your children to manage their energies from the heart at an early age. The earlier children understand the balance between their head and their heart, the less they will have to unlearn later in life in order to discover who they really are. The heart and head games are fun ways to introduce children to self-management and self- security.

Sexual Nurturing

As you balance your masculine and feminine energies, your electromagnetism increases. This brings heightened awareness and deepens your experience with all people and with life. As a man or woman balances the male and female aspects within their own system, they not only become more sensitive to their partner's deeper needs but also to their own. It results in a more *comprehen- sive* sensitivity to people and nature. This will increase the appeal of the future man and woman—mentally, emotionally, sexually, etc. Let's talk about that.

Male/female balance within yourself expands your sexual intelligence. Your increased sensitivity allows you to understand *the heart essence of sexual involvement,* beyond the *form* and the

---

*This book was originally entitled *Heart Smarts: Teenage Guide for the Puzzle of Life*, first edition published in June 1991.

parade. Once you develop heart sensitivity in sex, you tremendously enhance your nurturing capabilities. Heart sensitivity is about giving that caring respect that females often miss in the throes of things. Men need to remember to nurture a woman's wholeness while basking in the elixir. A large number of men today know this, but there are always deeper levels of care and understanding to be developed.

Nurturing can take place without physical contact, and physical contact often takes place without nurturing. Be careful not to confuse "nurturing" with "physical gratification aerobics." There is a difference. If not careful, you'll find yourself seeking union just to feed the ego insecurities. If you get too caught up in that, you will find yourself trying to take something via sex yet not giving it back. This causes ongoing male and female problems, but under the category of innocent ignorance. However, hiding behind innocent ignorance is about over. Increasing relationship awareness will require all individuals to become more responsible in their interactive involvements with other people.

A more conscious care for people is the remedy. Sex is powerful, but it is way more powerful on the *essence* level than the physical level, though the physical often is what it is! Understanding and experiencing sex at the essence level leads to a new dimension of care and appreciation for a much ill-managed and taken-for-granted gift. The essence level is where you deeply merge and bond mentally and emotionally rather than just on the physical level. A deeper appreciation for each other helps facilitate this essence level contact and integration.

When you experience essence communication, your whole system (mental, emotional and physical) is revitalized and energized with *sustained* effects. Many are not aware of the deeper levels of union possible between male and female. The mystery of sex needs to be unearthed and understood in its completion. Females especially are onto this, but so are many men.

Complete sex is way deeper than physical passion. It is *sensi-*

tivity and *care* that ring the loudest bell. The man of the future will go for the whole package—*nurturing* included—therefore yielding more meaningful fulfillment and completion. Most men and women are not purposefully insensitive to each other's needs; it's just that learning deeper respect and attunement is an unfolding growth process. With conscious effort, relationships can be brought into balance and maturity. It's worth the energy it takes because of the energy it saves.

I'm only sharing knowledge from my own experience that can speed up personal self-empowerment. It helped me tremendously. I'm not trying to dilute the invigoration of the male thrust in life. I'm just trying to add some sensitivity and texture to the process. Probably (possibly intentionally), there's a dash or two of macho in me; but I've also learned to be more sensitive and understanding (though I paid some dues in the learning process). I'm into the balance and empowerment of the complete man, not the sterilization of the male drive.

Soon, men and women will be pursuing information regarding the transformational power of balancing their individual male/female polarities. It has been talked about for years, but is just beginning to be put in streetsense terms that can translate into efficient results. People move fast when they realize there is power and efficiency to be gained by a new intelligence innovation...well, some do. All I am really referring to is the development of the total inner nature, which would have to increase the fun and quality in your co-creative experiences in life.

The Advantages of the Heart in Business

Successful businesses of the future will become wise to the importance of taking care of the people first—the employees, consumers, each other. Businesses will make many changes in order to take advantage of the new *family frequency momentum*. Smart businesses will learn to put their first emphasis on quality in relationships. Then product sales increases will be fun add-ons as a result of more *care*.

Times have changed. The planet is engaging in a "quality" revolution. Both people quality and product quality are in demand. Large corporations are now re-gearing to offer better quality because it is a must. People are quicker to realize when they are not getting it. If consumers can't get quality at one place, then another business will soon offer it down the street. Since *quality* is a new social buzzword and trend, realize that *sincerity in the people business is where real lasting quality is born*—not just from better-built consumer products. The first to understand the family way of dealing with people will become examples of quality relationships within businesses, social organizations, governments and at home.

The lack of male/female understanding in the business world, politics and social organizations alike, is causing a tremendous energy leak. In the coming years, most businesses will become "heart smart" in the name of *economy* (if they care to survive*).* The lack of adequate child care, medical insurance and family medical leave are business issues that are creating tremendous amounts of stress. *Stress* equals lost *dollars* on a business budget sheet. Sure people know that, but it hasn't been efficiently addressed yet. Still, it's happening—the dawning at least.

When caring for *people* gets the first consideration—before "lord dollar" gets his—then the efficiency which results from caring will tremendously boost the employee commitment, the loyalty and the profits.

Future successful businesses will be quick on their toes to provide proven systems of heart management and self-empowerment for their employees. If you harmonize the people first, then business will self-adjust with less friction, less stress. It hasn't always worked that way because greed has supplied the building blocks for profit, while capitalizing on the consumers' innocent ignorance.

Greed has had a good ride but it has run itself against the wall. An intelligent escape from the greed backwash would be:

returning to the heart in business. It's the backwash of stress that will scoot people off their tails and into their hearts much faster. More and more attention will soon be focused on the need to manage business from the heart, especially after executives figure out that the heart is the gateway to the mysterious intuition that everyone is looking for. Heart intelligence unfolds the intuition, providing clear business discrimination that results in profitable action.

Because of being checkmated by stress, businesses will eventually have to put consideration for the people first. A twisty realization will be when the business arena finds out that it is more profitable in dollars and cents to *care for the people first*. I call that "Intui-tech intelligence." Some will resist this approach at first. But watch how the next ten years in the rock tumbler of social consciousness will round out the maturity of business ethics and intentions.

Businesses are just a symbol of the coming changes. It's really the *individual* application of *self-management* that will cause mass transformation into another level of self-maturity and stress release.

I'm not trying to be an aspiring visionary. I'm just giving you an abbreviated sweep of the next decade's unfoldment. How do I know this to be true? Well, how do you know that I don't? There are many men and women on the planet that share these same views on the new business trends. It's obvious that the *family concept* will be the backdrop for the next level of communication and understanding in our society. Many businesses are already onto this, and so are many growth-sensitive people. We are only in the embryonic stages of this next long remaining trend—Back to the Family.

Love

LOVE is the creme essence of *efficient and caring action*. As you make efforts to balance your personal energy by following your heart, then more love is released through all aspects of your nature. Love acts as a *solvent* that dissolves the negative, while acting as a *tonic* to accent your positive—thereby increasing your overall quality of experience. In the future, people will practice loving more because they will wake up to the "smarts" that prove: *By loving and caring more, it's "your own tail" you're saving.* That's an efficient reason to love, but it's not selfish as it could seem. Love going out and coming back takes care of the *whole* and you are part of that.

Love is the most effective energy expenditure known to people, yet people know it not. When love goes out, it comes back—period. Mass consciousness has only explored the surface levels of intelligence that are hidden within the power of love. Humans have tried everything to solve the *stress overload*, except to practice loving more—a deeper active caring, in all business and relationships.

Many people are now starting to experience a new energy filtering down through the density of mass consciousness. This energy stirs your spirit to find freedom of expression and amplifies the voice within your heart. This new planetary energy facilitates people in thinking more about the *heart* and its potentials in all human affairs. At the same time, it can also accentuate the stress levels for people who continue to control their lives from the unmanaged head. Some have greater sensitivity to this energy influx than others—but give it time. You will see more people waking up to heart awareness than you've ever seen before. It's a time when humanity will get into the people business with more sincerity. This isn't a fairy tale promise. Sure, I'm aware of how tough it is out there, but heart intelligence is not an unapproachable reality.

People can find much stress release in the family feeling

experienced in support groups, study groups, workshops or among friends sharing. Many don't have time for that, but you may find it's worthy of your time and investment as stress keeps on increasing. When people gather together with *sincerity*, and are not just focused in their heads, then heart intuition opens up. This creates the feeling of family, which releases stress and gives birth to valuable insights for preventive maintenance. Group support expands your capacity to love, proving you can extend family past your immediate circle. Sincerely working with groups in mutual support is a gold mine waiting to be shared. Even if you don't think you need it, you can often be surprised at how much you gain from the experience. Experiment, give it a try. True bonding has always been a reservoir for nurturing.

If you want to extend your family feeling with a group of people but don't know where to start, first desire it in your heart. Then make inquiries and you're likely to draw to you the right people and situation for your needs. As you sincerely practice your own heart management, this creates energy magnetics which help draw to you your true heart's desires. There are always more people with whom you can resonate, and living from your heart can link you with them in fun and sometimes unusual ways.

The hub of human efficiency *is* the heart, be it in family or business. As heart intelligence unfolds, it will rekindle the warmth of the family concept. So, crank up your ol' Heart and start loving more. New social intelligence will prove that *care*, preceding action, is extremely economical. Sure, it takes a little practice but so does golf! It's better to live from the heart than to remain a "keeper of stress."

Sexual Harassment
A General Commentary

Women are "tired of it" and men are wondering, "What's all the fuss about?" What is fun to many men turns out to be harassment to the women. We obviously have a communication problem here. Sexual harassment is an issue that's affecting many people and increasing stress. Let's go behind the scenes of this growing social dilemma in order to better understand some of the root causes.

For many years now, we've lived in a male-dominant society which positions men as the icons of the planetary power structure. This may have served some assumed social purpose in the past, but it's the '90s now. Maturity and understanding need to adjust themselves to the awareness of the time. Respect and equality will be the result of this maturing process.

Any time there is a shift in consciousness, or when new intelligence is being instated on the planet, distortions occur in people's perceptions. This is intensified as people fight to the last straw to preserve the *securities* of old mind-sets and self-convenient patterns. But it's like the growing pains that kids go through.

You have to stretch at times to grow into the new.

It's often hard for people to change. For instance, years ago some fought against the abolition of slavery. Yet, since then, "time" has brought a deeper heart realization among society that slavery just wasn't balanced. In sexual harassment issues, we are not dealing with the crudeness of slavery, but we could be guilty of the *abrasiveness* of undeveloped sensitivity. As I've said before, men, as a whole, are not purposely insensitive. They are just in the transition of weaning from "old-school mind-sets" and attitudes. Many men still don't understand when something they thought was a casual remark turned out to be sexual harassment to a female listener.

In such encounters, the motive behind the remark could be innocent. However, at a deeper level of perception, the innocence could be founded on ignorance—a lack of understanding of the female system. In the new intelligence, even "innocent ignorance" will soon have to be educated—or it will meet with a new, more empowered resistance from the female race.

Many women have been stifled by the male-dominant society. As a result, some often approach the sexist issues with unbalanced ambition and spiked aggressions, therefore drawing fire from a threatened and surprised male species. Confusion and misunderstanding between the sexes is no longer hidden behind closed doors. Bringing the female/male problems out in the open is a major step towards finding resolution. The female and male communication gap won't be mended overnight but the wise can see the light of hope approaching.

The man of the future will be a man who has the awareness and balance of his feminine and masculine energy polarities within himself. As I've said, this will not threaten the men's *maleness factor;* it will tremendously *enhance it.* It's not a social "demotion" for men to realize that they have female and male polarities within them that need balancing; it is a personal advancement in intelligence and in empowerment.

Head-to-head stances and war-painted aggressions seem to be common modalities of negotiation on the sexual harassment issues at this time. This will tame down much as heart intelligence starts to guide humanity through an efficient co-creative balancing process. Some issues are changing through the process of *head bashing*, but real progress will not occur until issues are worked out at the *heart* level. Without heart communication, you can "make points" in one area and create more bitterness in another—never finding balance or mutual respect.

Sexual Harassment:
A Deeper Look for Both Sides

The balancing of female and male sexual issues in the workplace and in other social settings is an enlightening experience for both women and men in our society. It needs to be approached with more compassion and sensitivity from both sides.

Let's take an inside look at the male involvement in sexual harassment. Men say they didn't intend to cause sexual harassment in many accused situations. Often, men don't really know the depths of intimidation and inner anguish that certain comments and gestures put women through. As men develop the sensitive (feminine) side of their nature, they will no longer conveniently write off the harassment issues with: "What's the big deal," or "What's all the fuss about!" The intimidation and emotional anguish that women experience are a lot to fuss about and to be tired of.

The increase in media attention on workplace harassment, domestic abuse, date rape, etc., will force both sexes to grow up and balance both female and male qualities within their own individual natures. This will create the next level of power for men (and women) in business, politics and personal magnetics. Having a deeper hearing ability and more consideration does not diminish the male constitution of strength: It empowers it many times more! I'm not suggesting that men become submissive; nor do I mean that men have to think like women in order to bring their female polarity in balance with their male nature. It's no threat. It's future smarts—the emerging of the complete man.

Once men really start to understand that deeper sensitivity is an add-on to overall male magnetism, they'll be quick to get the feminine aspects of their nature in balance. Self-empowerment increases when: the nurturing aspect of a man is brought into *balance* with the "boys-will-be-boys" side of his nature.

Many men are now reluctant to make advances towards women, for fear that it will be labeled sexual harassment. If you're not sure how a woman is taking your advances, go deeper into your heart truth and try to change places (as best you can) with the female involved in the situation (without projecting the male sexual libido in the trade-off). As you make the effort to change places with the female, you might still tend to project how you think a woman *should* respond. Shift your focus from your head thoughts and emotions to your source of strength and care in the heart. Then sincerely ask your own heart intelligence to guide you. With practice, you will be able to place yourself in a woman's shoes with more sensitivity and understanding of how she really feels in those situations. Realize that if women are different from men on the outside, they're probably somewhat different in their inner responses as well.

If women and men both go to their hearts when assessing each other, they will get a sensitive and truer read-out of the other's nature. This could sound complex, but, with a sincere care and desire to know, new understandings will unfold as you make efforts. The increase of social intelligence is a growth and maturing process, no different from children growing through adolescence into adulthood. As people practice living more in their hearts, we will see true respect develop between the sexes and the issue of sex "superiority" will become nonexistent. The solutions will come in *the shaping up of the individual self,* and in learning to use *care* and *compassion* while communicating about female and male differences.

In earlier years, I thought I was sensitive, but it was only to defend my own point of view. I assumed that women were best at raising children and tidying up—the convenience format. I believed that female opinions were wimpy, so I would veto their say and have things my way. However, I started making progress as I made changes in myself rather than trying to rearrange the women. The most valuable asset I came out with was learning how to put myself in another's situation when making assessments and decisions.

The women I knew seemed to approach life differently from men. I wanted to understand why their reactions to situations were so often opposite to my own. I started by trying to listen to women without running my own mind tapes of male ego assumptions and expectations—the standard male approach. Soon I was able to quit assuming and generalizing. My effort to develop sensitivity and to care and respect women more didn't diminish my maleness. It gave it much more balance and completeness.

Women are way worth "finally" getting to know.

Men are obviously important but the difference is this: They already know it and society confirms it! Women only want the same freedom to have their worth and creative expression acknowledged. The women are not trying to take over, they are only asking the men to *move over* and share the future. Men and women will be glad to ride "white horses" together once they realize how efficient for the whole that could be. The fun co-creation of the *two* is what can spiral planetary consciousness into a new dimension of communication efficiency.

Neither sex is smarter, they just have different contributions for the whole and life is waiting for the merging of female and male potentials to gel and result in more human efficiency. Women can expedite this process if they approach the feminist issues from the heart—with compassion and understanding, yet being firm when firm needs be. This will add more potency and intelligence to the integrity of their appeal for equality. If women approach these issues from the *head*, they will only be trying to get even or prove a point, which is like adding gasoline to fire—it ignites the male reactive ego nature.

Women, more and more, will realize their security has to come from their own hearts. You can't wait for men, jobs or issues to change before you get security inside. Self-security doesn't mean that you act as if sexual harassment and male intimidation don't exist. It does mean that you can keep yourself from being drained on the mental and emotional levels until you can change those uncomfortable situations.

People accept the fact that females and males are different physically. Because of hormonal differences they also have different psychological perspectives. After there's mutual understanding of the basic differences, then the next level of cooperative respect can be developed. This next level is sensitive because it involves *giving,* rather than just looking for stimulation or attention from the other. This means giving time and care while cultivating a more sincere listening ability. True giving doesn't require stimulation in return or pat itself on the back for having endured a conversation. If you attempt to give while pre-occupied with having to endure, you dilute your good intentions.

Many women feel they make sincere efforts to listen to men even when the topic of conversation is not their cup of tea or their flavor of stimulation. Yet women often feel restricted in sharing what's important to them. With a wave of the hand or a few dismissing words like, "Hush, the ball game score's coming on," women are often silenced. Then, what makes it worse is women know that if they ever used "power dismissals" in communicating to men, it would be a natural invitation to World War III—or something formidable. Knowing this can create repression and a form of psychic imprisonment.

Men are not always deliberately trying to repress women, they're just being traditionally male. Understand that there's an innocent insensitivity involved which can be educated as men attempt to make a deeper connection with their nurturing side. It's understandable why some women would be bitter and retaliate. Though anger has served as a good wake-up call, it's not the most efficient method for achieving the next phase of completion in balancing the female and male differences. I think that most people, by now, are starting to awake, but they don't know from which side of the bed to depart. The next step is more care and compassion and an effort to understand the differences in each other's make-up. Women and men are equal in what they have to contribute. The heart is the fulcrum for balancing this social seesaw.

A Look at the Women's and Men's Movements: Working Issues Out at the Heart Level

A while back, the feminist movement seemed like it had run its course, and without as much accomplished as many would have liked. Well, it's not over. That momentum towards equality wasn't wasted because its intention was worthy and part of an unfolding blueprint for future efficiency.

In the beginning of the feminist movement, some women erupted like a fiery volcano with seemingly unbridled assertion. But realize, much of that was because men didn't seem to *hear or respond* to anything other than charged expressions. Maybe some women did come on strong in the beginning of the female unearthing process, but it was a necessary *re-action,* rather than just an aggressive *action.* Repression is like a boil that finally pops when the pressure is not relieved and women have been repressed for ages.

Over the years, factions developed within the women's movement, creating cross-frequencies which seriously diluted its potentials for achieving equality. Some women can get so ambitious in proving they can "outdo" men, that they cut off their nurturing qualities and become unbalanced. This won't achieve fulfillment or equality and can even make matters worse.

At this time, large percentages of women don't identify with or see advantages in what has been the feminist approach. They don't even want to be associated with the feminist label. This is because they sense, consciously or subconsciously, the imbalance and the lack of heart and inclusive overview in many of the issues and approaches. Until a chord of resonance is struck that touches the hearts of women en masse, most will remain passive and non-participating. It's not because they're wimps, or don't care, or that the issues aren't relevant—they're just intuitively waiting for a more *complete* approach. When it arrives, it will create heart resonance and more women will participate with genuine enthusiasm.

The feminist movement is now in the process of reshaping itself. A new minority vision is being born which will gain populist support because of the refinement of the vision to include what's important to the *whole*—family, community, men, as well as women. As I've said before, I'm not limiting the term "family" to women at home raising children or to an immediate family nest. I'm talking about an active family warmth extended to female/male issues, social and political concerns, the workplace, etc.

Reactive, aggressive focus just on sexual politics can create an imbalance of male frequencies within the individual female nature. This will balance out for many women as the coming new movement swells in strength because of including the deeper concerns for *all* in its efforts. Some who participated in the old feminist agendas (who have acknowledged their own inner maturing process) are now beginning to come forth again, envisioning and speaking of a broader concept of feminism that embraces the *whole*. They will help to fashion the unfoldment of the new and effective trends. Sure, there will be resistance, but these women will become secure in their intuitive understanding that they are on the right track. They will need to follow their hearts and not let social pressure dilute their knowingness and commitment.

As social awareness increases, more people will realize that the new approach is not abandoning the feminist cause—it's empowering the cause and taking it to its next level of fulfillment. It's been thirty years or more of awakening and gridwork, but, like a rocket, the old stages have to be released to move into the new horizons. Intuitive, heart-based breakthroughs will act as a booster rocket in this transition. The ultimate movement (or highest stage of the rocket) will take off when women *and* men work together to create a single movement—new equality-based consciousness. In the near but reluctant future, both sexes will come to the clear realization that: *balance* can be achieved through heart communication much more quickly than through resistance and retaliation.

As long as the female/male relationship equilibrium remains unbalanced, stress will continue to be the "backwash." It will still be "bite and scratch" for a while, but the mind can make it seem worse than it is. (Much of the extra pain, unfortunately, comes from one's own self.) Today, more women (and men) are putting their vulnerability on line by telling their true feelings outside the closets of repression and fear. Heart sincerity in communication creates a deeper hearing ability in society, not to mention the increase in true empowerment that it gives you.

As I've said, the *head* approach to female/male issues will only sustain separatism and non-constructive competition. The solid *heart* approach will lead to an appreciation of equality and all of its creative possibilities for the whole. Learn to take a *stand* from the heart, and not a *stance* from your head. Then any efforts toward a cause will result in a much higher ratio of accomplishment.

As women develop their own heart security, they multiply their *power* to change situations or peacefully adapt until they can. It's not a sacrifice to operate from the heart—it's actually a lot easier. As distortions are resolved, women and men will look at each other as buddies with different qualities, co-creating efficiency and fulfillment together. This is not a pipe dream. It's about an awakening after a long sleep.

The matured and self-secured man in the future will not even want to be associated with the stigmatized and dated structure of a male-dominant society. It will be beneath his intelligence level to think that way. Men will gain tremendously from the balanced integration of women into the planning rooms of life.

Women are still sparse in the major board rooms and seats of decision. This is not necessarily because men are selfish in maintaining positions of power. It's because of the mind-sets of our traditional society. The integration of women into planning rooms is new to men as a whole, and newness tends to create threat and over-sensitivity until the dust settles. Women will need to respect male sensitivity in this unfolding process, just as they are wanting more sensitivity and respect for themselves. Female and male energies each have essential parts of the puzzle. A heart approach from both will help enlighten the differences and create an excellent (joint) adventure. Both female and male are too intelligent to be *rated* and *sub-rated*. It's a time for women and men alike to de-agonize their differences and unify their efforts.

As consciousness increases in this decade, many more people will start to realize: it's stupid and sub-intelligent to think that women who are qualified shouldn't be executives, or shouldn't have political seats and corporation seats. I'm not implying that for every man in business or politics that there should be a woman. I am saying that it shouldn't be a threat and shouldn't matter. Let the qualifications of the moment decide who or what would be the best for the situation.

A Look at the Men's Movement

Public attention to the growing, new men's movement is now on the increase. Like the women's movement, there are different attitudes and positions taken by men in trying to decide which agenda will have the most worth. This is creating divisions, bickering and self-righteousness among some men. The men's movement is primarily a search for male identity, a more complete sense of self, while the women's movement has focused on the need for external changes in society to give women more freedom, equality and completeness. The trends of both movements are leading towards a new, balanced empowerment for both sexes.

The subliminal prompting of the men's movement, whether people are yet conscious of it or not, is a desire to balance the male/female polarities within men to reach completeness. The masculine polarity is the warrior-confidence side of men and some groups are primarily trying to develop this side to find balance. Other men's groups are working on developing the feminine polarity, the nurturing side of their nature. In both groups, men often spend time sharing feelings and deepening communication. Some support the feminist movement to help women achieve equality.

A third perspective is beginning to emerge with the recognition that the men's movement needs to unite the best approaches of all the men's groups. People are born with different hormonal blueprints that indicate the general mental, emotional and physical ways they respond to life's issues. In their quest for balance and completeness, they would naturally have different opinions and divisions. If all participants would respect each other's agendas, based on being natured differently, this would be an effort towards the development of the complete man. The female and male polarities come together and find a balanced synthesis in the heart. That's where you become the complete person or true human being.

The important point is that more men are now trying to get in deeper contact with their individual selves, which is the first step in what I call waking up and becoming complete. The HeartMath system can facilitate both the women's and men's movements in finding balance and direction. People will eventually discover that the heart is the balance point for achieving any particular goal they are trying to reach. It's through the heart that these movements will grow up and become united in their efforts to uplift the intelligence of the planetary whole. It's really all one group anyhow. Women and men just have their own ways of breaking through crystallized patterns into new levels of self-awareness. Even after breaking through old patterns, men and women will still find it beneficial and empowering to meet separately to deepen their bond of mutual resonating support.

Learning the hard way is not always the most productive way, though some believe that it is. Becoming heart smart keeps you from always having to learn the hard way. When people learn to operate from heart discrimination and govern their own energies, most of the female/male problems will wilt along with the outdated structures of business and society in general. Both women and men have seriously unexplored potentials that won't ever manifest until they blend together to form a third force—higher creative manifestation and a gateway into Intui-Technology. Our social systems will then move into a new dimension of effectiveness. Let's explore the new forthcoming vitality of equality and co-creation, while putting outdated, non-efficient structures to rest.

Ego-Economics

So what's Ego-Economics? I'm glad you're curious. Ego-Economics is what you experience when your ego gets to have *fun*—yet you don't lose heart direction or self-management in the process. There are various related terms for the concept of ego economy which are already in use. Faith Popcorn calls it "Egonomics" in her book *The Popcorn Report*—a fun and insightful perspective into the forthcoming changes in the "people business."

To experience ego-economics, you don't repress your ego enjoyment; you learn to balance and manage it. Without balance, the ego drive often causes tremendous amounts of non-efficient energy expenditure. It can cause you energy deficits as it plunges ahead with unbridled assertion. Your heart intelligence has the capacity to balance and fulfill your ego nature. As you practice managing your attitudes from the heart, you unfold a harmonious synthesis between your ego and the rest of your inner nature.

I realize that different philosophies have various interpretations of what is called "ego." Most definitions represent the ego personality as a conglomeration of unmanaged mind and emotions that seem to take on a life of their own. They can result in self-centered, self-righteous, vain attitudes and behavior as well as inverted ego—poor-self-image, etc. The ego nature is part of the personality structure, but tends to spin off on its own without heart management. When balanced, your ego creatively expresses your innate spirituality.

Many have believed that you need to annihilate the ego to achieve peace or enlightenment. Let's look at the ego as an important part of your nature, just as the mind and emotions are—when unmanaged they all create stress feedback and block the flow of light from your spirit. The unmanaged mind can make you miserable. But you don't destroy the mind; you refine and manage it. The emotions can make misery worse, but you don't eliminate the emotional nature; you bring it under management and realize it's a gift. The ego is not bad; it just needs to be balanced and managed like the other aspects of your nature.

Other than surface participation, many people avoid religions or spiritual movements because they often repress the ego nature. People are tired of feeling guilty about their ego. Inside themselves they innately know that their ego nature is where much of their fun and individuality is experienced. Ego repression has to stop before any system of peace can effectively dissipate stress overloads. It's managing the ego from your inner source of power that gives it fulfillment and completion.

The ego expresses itself in society everywhere you turn, though many try to hide their ego expression behind plastic humility. (That's an inverted ego trip, the opposite of a righteous attitude.) Realize it's your ego nature that registers the fun of a party, of sports, of business, of romance, of spiritual festivities, etc., etc. Healthy ego fun nurtures your whole system. Respect other people's ego enjoyments because, whatever your belief structures are, you have your own *ego food* of some kind. It's easy to justify and qualify your own ego enjoyments, while being quick to judge and criticize others for theirs.

People are nourished by different things at different times in their lives and that's the prerogative of their own unfoldment. Something that's efficient and fun for you may not be efficient or fun for the next person. A hamburger may be more nourishing for a logger than a meatless dish. (There are always exceptions.) For some, a vegetarian dish may be more nourishing than meat. If you think you have knowledge that would help others make better choices, then share it with them, if appropriate, but without the judgments. That's tricky because: *Each time you change perspectives in life, it's hard not to measure other people by your new standards and beliefs.* When you have respect for the choices and views of others, that facilitates their growth. I'm not saying you have to agree with their views, but respect their process of unfoldment.

Think of how many times in the past you just "knew what you knew was right." Now, realize how many times your perspectives have changed as the years have passed. Why wouldn't others have a right to go through changes as you did and will continue to do? Once you understand this, you'll realize it doesn't make sense to keep your inner flexibility frozen with judgments. By remembering that most people's truths mature over time, it helps overcome the tendency to judge other people's ego expressions. When you see someone making what seems to be an unproductive ego choice, have compassion and understanding—that's what you would want for yourself.

Different Strokes for Different Folks

In ego-economics, there are different ego appetites and fulfillment levels. Some people want a house and white picket fence, a dog and the bills paid. Others may have an ego appetite for big business and many houses in exotic places. That's okay...different strokes. Being effective and a good person doesn't mean you have the same preferences or ego fulfillment blueprint as everyone else.

By following your heart and being true to yourself, you will draw to yourself your balanced fulfillment.

People are often so identified with money and glitter that they can't discern what would be their most fulfilling ego expression and fun. Money and luxury are not negative. They are neutrals which people qualify either as negative or positive, depending on their heart motives and personal energy management. Poor people can be as out of touch with their hearts as rich people. Your inner peace is based on your self-management and adaptability—not your monetary gain. People either have self-management or they don't; neither their riches nor their poverty is the issue. Heart intuition can unravel your ego complexities and unfold the direction in life that would be the most rewarding.

If you're a big dreamer and like big productions, then go for the "whole farm." There's nothing wrong with enjoying your creations and achievements without feeling guilty. Don't let the envy of others drag you down; they have their own growing up to do. It's okay to go-for-it—just stay heart-managed in the process. Learn to think in a limitless way—meaning don't box yourself in with thoughts of what you can't do and can't have.

An efficient move in the chess game of life is to first make peace with your existing conditions—rich or poor, overweight or underweight, etc., etc. As the heart adapts to what *is*, it releases the intuition that can help you better understand your situation. By adapting, I'm not saying you shouldn't try to improve your conditions. I'm just saying your heart smarts give you more efficient directions for making wise changes than an unmanaged *head approach*. If you go against the grain of your heart feelings while trying to better your life, your head can lead you deeper into the abyss. Heart energy magnetizes what would truly be better for you.

The head often fools people into thinking that *ungoverned* ego satisfaction is the highest of human treats (with the attitude of "eat, drink and be merry for tomorrow you may die"). Society's stress overloads prove that's not the most sensible attitude. In the name of fun and stimulation, people carelessly make fun of others with slant humor and judgmental gestures. If ego-stimulation isn't governed by the *heart*, you create stress and shallow relationships.

You can accuse powerful personalities of being on an ego trip, while being on as big a one yourself but in less public settings. Jealousies cause heavy-handed judgments towards famous people and influential figures. It's time to allow and appreciate all. One of the most efficient things you can do in the ego-economy business is to leave people alone and clean up your own backyard. Let that be your first good deed for the whole, if you're interested in helping.

Most people don't care to live for the good of the whole unless they can have *fun* doing it. When applying *ego-economy,* you get your true fun without losing your heart connection and balance in the process. This true, complete fun I speak of originates from your heart and is largely experienced and expressed in your ego nature. Heart-inspired fun uses the ego to express your love and care. Then you can freely enjoy the adventure of life without getting over-stressed in return. Your ego-enjoyment gets nurtured along with your inner spiritual aspirations. They all become one and the same; there's no separation. Infuse your ego with spirit and become your complete self. It's self-balance and simply learning to be yourself that makes this possible.

Being Yourself

Many people are locked out from being themselves because of having to live up to vanity standards imposed by the social pressures of society. For instance, certain people tend to be overweight due to the biological make-up of their particular glandular system. Because of social pressure concerning diet, they spend their lives trying to live up to other people's measurements of approval. In being yourself, you have to first adjust to whatever cards you were dealt in life and attempt to make peace with that. Then, if you want to make changes, use technology, disciplines, systems, etc., to explore your possibilities. However, if your results don't stack up to other people's demands or expectations, you still need to make efforts to accept and be yourself. This will save you from an overload of turmoil. You can be happier with self-acceptance than with trying to live up to others' perceptions of how you should be. People really know this inside, but still tend to let social standards dictate their level of inner peace.

Until you learn to manage your thought patterns and emotions, you can still create inner turbulence by not meeting up to your own expectations. Much stress is released by developing compassion for yourself. Nature designed you with the capacity to be happy even if you have biological limitations. When living from the heart, you transcend your own and other people's judgments of handicaps and shortcomings. Many have testified to this truth time and again. When the light of the heart is lit, you add spark to your environment regardless of personal limitations. When you mechanically rely on other people and things for security, you slow down the process of becoming *you*. Let others facilitate, but not dictate your identity in the adventure of life.

The process of being yourself is accelerated as you realize that it's you who can complete your efforts—or not. It's you who chooses poor self-image or not; it's you who allows your past to drain your present experience; it's you who can contact higher facilitation through your heart rather than trying to figure it all out from the head—and it's you who can stop those energy leaks in your system. Your intuition will guide you in becoming your true self and not just a self-defeating imitation.

Realize that within your heart there is the strength to regulate all the choices in life. *Following your heart is a major key to being your true self and builds the confidence to express your full potential.* Most people don't function at their highest capacity because they approach learning by pursuing external knowledge rather than by drawing from their inner knowingness. External knowledge facilitates but doesn't really draw forth your full spectrum of creative potentials. Only you can discover what's right for you.

Being yourself deeply connects you with a steady source of confidence and power to achieve. The more you are true to yourself, the more stress-free life you live. That's ego-economics.

9

Religions, New Age, Old Age, Any Age, "The NOW Age"

Crises such as earthquakes, floods, fires, etc., seem to unite communities in a *heart* effort to work for the good of the whole. Often these people are from totally different religious backgrounds, yet they work together like family in a catastrophe, forgetting their ranks and affiliations in life. By the end of the crisis, they've become so spiritually and emotionally bonded, they often decide to get together and commemorate the touching ordeal they've experienced.

As they become friends, they realize that they are a mixture of Christians, Jews, Buddhists, new agers, atheists, fortune tellers and traveling salesmen. They feel a family bonding, realizing that all are connected at the heart level. The point I am making is this: They experience the *family connection* regardless of their status, spiritual preferences or vanity structures. Unfortunately, it usually takes a catastrophe to synchronize that many diversified people in the heart at one time.

Status, cultural and religious differences stifle the true heart connections between people on the planet. (Unless there is a catastrophe, of course.) Do you ever wonder why catastrophes seem to be on the increase? Maybe it's "Mother Earth's" way of nudging people into realizing that we are all family and should create the experience of love in her yard.

Self-righteousness and vanity structures often keep people from realizing we are all one big family sharing one big yard, the Earth. Stress will finally cause people to relate to each other at the heart level. Spontaneous love will one day govern human relationships, not judgmental mind-sets or separative attitudes. You don't have to experience a catastrophe to evoke more sincere loving and caring for all. Just practice living from the heart—and send out what you expect back.

Old age or new age—religions will eventually mature to the point where they will replace judgments with love. A way to advance within your religious belief structure is to attend to your own self-management and leave others alone—until you can approach people through non-judgment and without attempting to re-arrange their worlds to suit your perceptions. Love the divinity in people and allow them to be different.

Humanity needs to be in the people business, rather than supporting separatism generated by non-efficient ego-stances. The spiritual wise men and women of the past were probably in the *people business*, but their followers tend to forget that as time passes. Many good-willed intentions lose their *heart essence* along the way. This is due to over-identity with the *structures* and *formats*. In my opinion, this could explain the strained vitality of religions and spiritual paths today—too much parade and not enough sincerity.

A Look at the New Age

The "New Age" is presently on *hold* while the "Now Age" is about to have its time. The Now Age is the age of individual (do-it-yourself) enlightenment—*Now!* Until this is implemented, stress will casually rule. The Now Age will not be ushered in by crystals, fairies or gurus. You finally have to "do it yourself" after the dust settles from the glitter, the glamour and the noise of each new parade that comes into town. I've experienced both new age and old age structures but decided it was more efficient to live in the "now." By the "now," I mean: *this moment.*

The one thing that *especially* challenges the tolerance level of many new agers is what some perceive as self-righteous, boxed-in viewpoints of fundamentalist religions. However, over a period of time (though not intentionally), many new agers reached the same point of self-righteousness and condescension as many fundamentalist groups. Then there was an over-exposure to new age glitter and postponed promises, which finally overloaded the public.

Now, much of the new age population is avoiding being identified with "new age." Many new age businesses have closed their doors, while other new age businesses are on the increase. Even though much of the general public has been turned off by aspects of the new age demeanor, they are still looking for new ways to cope with increasing stress and the changes occurring in society. The new age movement is undergoing a refining process along with the other basic religious structures.

People are tired of religious noise. They want to see an example of a system of self-management which will lighten the load of this planetary "stress-mess." There are many good people in different groups and religions, but most spiritual systems are missing a consistent infusion of Spirit. It's through your heart that this infusion can take place. Your heart feelings and commitment are what keep spiritual ideals and rituals alive.

Living from the heart can open the doorway to individual enlightenment, the manifestation of your true spirit into your day-to-day life. If you want to experience this, you can't escape being responsible for your own energy management—even if you are an ambassador of the new age or personal friends with the messiah of any particular religion.

A major handicap to enlightenment is that many of the different spiritual organizations insist that their way is the most effective way. This causes crystallized mind-sets and separation, complicating the realization that we are all one big family. The *Now* age is a humble gathering of old age and new age, like two fussy kids in a family who need a talking to. Life will soon explain to both old and new religions that separatism will not create the peace and enlightenment that people are looking for. We all need to learn a way to cooperate harmoniously regardless of spiritual preference. This can be achieved by relating to each other openly and sincerely from the heart—the family approach.

In my own maturing process, I learned much from orthodox religions and from new age ideas. Still, my heart directives call the shots on how I live. I don't care if *make-sense* comes from a person, a tree, or a sunset. I utilize it if it checks out in my own heart.

For example: I have read intelligent statements in a lot of books, but statements that Christ made especially intrigued me with their efficiency and foresight in the people business. Statements such as "Love ye one another;" "Do unto others as you would have them do unto you;" etc. To me, these statements imply that the prescription for peace and fulfillment is within the heart. Christ stressed the value of love and of loving each other.

In reading, I noticed that some followers of Christ had a tendency to judge on occasion. They found Christ chatting with the cheaters of the townspeople and couldn't understand why. He was probably illustrating to the followers something that many possibly haven't understood yet: He was in the "people business," not the judgment and self-righteousness business. Religions talk about purifying the mind from judgments and the sensory pulls of humanness. When the spirit is *not* flowing through your heart, your sensory appetites get amplified by the mind and create clouds of illusion. When the spirit flows through your heart, then the qualities of spirit (love, peace, non-judgment, wisdom, etc.) illuminate the mind and transform the body, making them instruments of divine intelligence from the Source. It's not just an abstract theory—it really can be done with sincere commitment and practice. Don't underestimate your potentials. Just make connection through the heart with your spirit and Source.

Religious structures facilitate many people, but, like the rest of our systems, they could stand a good dose of renewed vitality and inoculation with a non-judgment vaccine. Practicing deeper love and care for all people is a good way to activate this regenerative process. I'm not peddling any particular religious or spiritual path, but my favorite radio station is the still small voice inside. Like anyone else, I have to re-set the dial when it gets off into unmanaged mind static and out-of-the-heart programs.

Choosing a religious affiliation is a matter of heart resonance. The real strength of a church or group is built on the true bonding and heart resonance between its members. People have to decide what resonates with them and respect others' choices at the same time.

As simple as it sounds, your fulfillment can be hidden in the unfoldment of your heart intelligence. Understanding the working relationship between the head and the heart has helped me discriminate the differences between the doubtful mind talk and the voice of wisdom in the heart. I love people, yet I don't have to dance to other people's inharmonious music either. Neither do you and that's what this book is about—Self-empowerment. That's learning to respect other people's music, but dance to your own tune as you master harmony within yourself.

The *NOW* Age

The mounting stress proves that something is still missing in our spiritual and scientific systems of people facilitation. *"Now"* is the time when spiritual adolescence needs to step forward into a matured understanding of human relationships and communication. The Now Age is the age of *doing*! It will be hard to produce new ethics more efficient than treating people the way you would like to be treated—all people, not just your pet particulars. Expand your care to more and more people.

If you are involved in a religion or a spiritual path and want to help the planet, then purge the backwash in your own religious system first. This will add potency to your outreach. Judgmental stances will have to be transformed through love and care before any system will experience the revival that many have long awaited and seriously need. It's time for all systems on the planet— spiritual, political, social and personal—to clean up their own backyards at last, rather than just decorate the front lawn.

Heart intuition offers hope for a workable relationship between the different belief structures on the planet. Human intelligence has only scratched the surface of understanding *the inner heart*. Even the physical heart and what makes it beat is a big enough mystery to science. Through researching the relationship between head and heart frequencies, science will uncover a new dimension of understanding regarding human nature and its functions.

Peace and efficiency are always only a few intuitions away. Intuition can be steadily developed by learning to attune to your heart and become buddies with your inner knowingness. As you practice deeper listening, you'll find you can easily distinguish your heart feelings from *head* chatter. Practice with even half the perseverance that you would use in learning music or aerobics. Personal security and stress release will result from your efforts. That inner voice must have been intended for something—*like directions for balanced living*.

Self-empowerment is not intended to threaten or compete with any other system. It's about people becoming themselves. Attend to yourself and the rest of the world will prosper from that.

Summary:
Important Points to
Remember and
Practice

This book can affect people in different ways because people have their own individual *frequencies of perception*. You can know something and categorize it in your mind with the intention of acting on it, but then go for months forgetting to bring those intentions into practical reality. Remember, remedies to problems may appear idealistic to one, yet be realistic to another. Practice can bring an ideal into reality.

Considering that the heart has *intelligence* could seem as unrealistic to some people today as the idea of a "BIC" lighter would have been to a caveman rubbing sticks to start a fire. If following the heart sounds too simple and easy—it is, once you know how. People who ride bikes know it's easy, but beginners perceive it as difficult. Though the concepts are simple, this book stands to become more useful to people as stress increases.

There are many people who already are successfully practicing following their heart. It's effective for them, but no more effective than you can make it for yourself. HeartMath organizes the "how-to-do's" and helps you remember what you intended to do. Because of survival living, many people often don't *apply* what they already know inside to their day-to-day interactions with others and the environment. My experience is that if people apply even a fourth of what they know, they'll discover a new level of freedom and quality in life.

You can benefit from practicing and discussing the deeper understandings of heart potentials in a supportive group setting. As people support each other and bond at the heart level, it creates a nurturing environment. This is regenerative and can facilitate mental, emotional and physical healing. Sincere sharing prevents static buildup in an individual's system. Heart-to-heart communication is effective therapy and serves as preventive maintenance.

If you decide to practice the suggestions in this book by yourself, then re-read portions at a time as your intuition elects. Re-reading will help you remember to apply, and sincere application is what yields the benefits. The quality of your life is determined by what you do, not by what you know.

The following is a summary of key points for your review.

1. It may be helpful to re-read CHAPTER 2 for a deeper understanding of the difference between the head and the heart. They each have important functions. Many people direct their lives from the *head,* thinking it's their heart. Check it out, sincerely. Head thoughts which are qualified by the heart result in wisdom—wise decisions.

2. Practice listening more attentively for your heart's guidance. Use it to manage your head and balance your system. In practicing, you will tend to vacillate back and forth in your understanding and efforts, as you do while learning golf, tennis, computer programming, or anything. Keep on making efforts to develop sensitivity to your heart intuition. This will help create a

joint venture between your head and your heart. The balance between the two can eliminate tremendous amounts of stress in your day-to-day environment.

3. Try practicing heart management first with simple issues. Then you'll increase your ability to use heart power in all decisions in life. As you minimize your stress accumulation, it slows down the aging process, allowing you more fun and vitality. It doesn't take a long time to see the benefits if you make a heart commitment.

4. Overcare depletes a large portion of a person's daily individual energy allotment. Re-read CHAPTER 3 on Care and Overcare because understanding how not to go over the line into overcare plays an important part in the management of your personal energies. Remember—there's not enough true care in most people's lives, but way too much overcare. Find a true balance by closely observing yourself. Discover your overcares and stop those energy leaks from draining your system.

5. The energy that you save from not overcaring can be used to overcome obstacles that before you couldn't. Learn not to cry over "spilt-milk" of the past. You can't bring back the crop that was killed by rain or drought. You can start anew, because what else is there. You've heard of "release-and-let-go." It's facing life from the *heart* perspective that gives people the power to do that. Practice approaching people, places and issues from the heart and avoid unnecessary stress. If you sincerely practice the management of overcare, you'll start saving energy right in the moment.

6. If you're in pressured circumstances which you can't change, the heart attitude can give you power to more peacefully adapt to the situation. Maintaining heart perspective magnetizes facilita-

tion that often wouldn't have seemed possible. It's time to stop blaming other people for your problems. The balance of the head and heart energies gives you the power to change your perspective to gain a clear view. It's your perspective of a situation that holds you back and creates much of your excess stress. It's not the people or circumstances as much as you may think.

7. People have searched forever for a system of bottom-line mental and emotional management, yet it is within the heart of each person waiting to be used. That would make it fair and give hope to all people.

8. Learn to Freeze-Frame. When you experience anxiety, emotional overload, fear, disappointment, etc., practice *stilling* your emotions and mind processors. Stillness is best achieved by shifting your attention from the head thoughts and *focusing your energies* in your heart area for a few minutes. This is *Freeze-Framing*. It's "chilling out" so you can take an objective look at a situation. Anxiety can be managed more than you know with sincere effort from the heart.

As you practice Freeze-Framing from the heart, you *can* temporarily stop the emotions and thoughts from clouding your capacity to see clearly. To make heart contact easier, relax as you Freeze-Frame and have compassion for yourself, or send someone or a child loving thoughts. This brings your attention to the heart area and diverts the focus of energy from your problems. Freeze-Frame dissipates the emotional charge, giving you a clear and objective perspective on the issue at hand. Clear perspective allows for creative and intuitive solutions. Freeze-Framing won't necessarily solve all your problems on the spot, but it helps you stop and see more potentials—which is the first step in finding answers.

When day-to-day mental and emotional stressors arise, make efforts to Freeze-Frame even if for a few minutes at first. More effort, more gain. Realize that intelligent solutions can often pop up quickly. Intuition works at a much faster speed than deduction when you are inwardly still enough for it to translate into your consciousness. Use an Intui-technique—practice Freeze-Framing before you make any major decision and you will develop the capacity to make wiser choices in all areas of life. Many times, the application of one Freeze-Framing can save you days and weeks worth of mental and emotional misery. It gives you a chance to *see* and act rather than just react, resulting in more efficient decisions.

Don't be discouraged in your first attempts; be gently persistent. Unmanaged thoughts and emotions can be the most exhaustive predators that you ever have to face in life. People already age fast enough without rushing it due to the lack of mental and emotional management. Managing these areas will be realized in the future as a most *practical* approach to the "fountain of youth."

9. Find your security within your own heart, not in other people, places or things. It can come from practicing heart management if you seriously want it. *Self-security* is your insurance for not being drained by the drama of life's events. Your favorite people in life are apt to let you down at times. When you become secure in your own heart, your life force isn't drained by disappointments in other people. Your heart realizes that everyone is vulnerable to non-efficient choices in life, so learn not to build your security on expectations of others. Heart intelligence shoots for the positive, but doesn't have a major setback when things don't always go as planned. It efficiently adapts, making it easier to find another solution. Life doesn't always present events exactly the way you would want them. That's why self-security is so important. Self-Security = Self-Empowerment!

10. Play a fun game by creating an imaginary budget sheet of your mental and emotional energy expenditures, like people do

with their financial expenditures. For one week, observe the amount of time that you spend involved in insecurities, overcares, resentments, anxiety, depression, poor self-image, hurt feelings, etc. It would shock people to realize how one hurt feeling or resentment can create hours of head processing and much mental and emotional pain.

Nagging mind chatter depletes people more than they know, and science is increasingly proving this to be true. Constant negative thoughts and emotions affect your system in the same way that burning trashy gas affects a car—it finally breaks down by the roadside. People are more conscious of their diet these days, but their mental and emotional junk often adds more stress to their system than junk food. When people get as conscious of their mental and emotional food quality as they are their physical food, planetary peace will then advance and so will health.

Create a mental and emotional *budget sheet* of how you spend your energies in the same way you calculate the dollars you spend or the calories you eat. Learn to change your deficits into assets in life and collect the dividends—fun living.

11. Inner-Ecology. Support the ecological movement, but don't lose sight of the bottom line task—the cleaning up of our inner environment so that the outer environment can be dealt with under intuitive direction with lasting effects. Until people manage themselves, the Earth will always be at risk—even with recycling bins on every corner. It's the mental and emotional debris floating in the earth's atmosphere (oZonk?) that causes people not to respect the ecology in the first place. That *clean-up* needs mass attention and adjustment. This will lead to balance for the Earth and its inhabitants.

12. Judgments, self-beating, guilt, hate, resentments, condescension, separatism and more—all of these have to Go! They leach our capacity to help each other and ourselves. Watch your-

self closely and weed these non-efficient attitudes and mind-sets out of your system by replacing them with an infusion of love and compassion. If you can't quite replace a resentment with love or compassion, you can at least make efforts to *neutralize* or dissipate non-productive thoughts and feelings. This stops the energy drain in your system. Science has already proven that churning judgments and resentments can result in health problems and disease. It's time for people to turn to common sense strategies to relieve stress and create their own peace.

13. Remember the *Family concept*—a more sincere care for all people—at home, in business, in social and political issues—and especially for yourself. Relating to people from the heart creates the family frequency which in turn creates harmony in your environment. The word "family" has love, care, warmth, compassion, forgiveness, non-judgment and cooperation tucked within its meaning. Just like you, other people have their own mind-sets and ceilings to break through. If you make more sincere efforts to *care* at deeper levels, that will make it easier for everyone to let go of draining attitudes and crystallized mind patterns.

Care is a major ingredient in the recipe for peace within yourself, your community and the planet. If you feel that you already care, then go deeper, *care more* and find the next level. Care is enlightening and leads to personal fulfillment if you would dare to believe there is such as that. There is! Cash in on the family frequency by extending your care and sincerity to larger numbers of people and experience the true profits of quality in life.

14. As more men and women learn to balance the male and female aspects within their individual natures, it will increase our ability to understand and respect each other. That will help bring about the natural realization of equality. It's the blending of the male and female energies in the planning rooms that results in the best for the whole—whether in family, business or social

reform. Remember the importance of nurturing and how deeper listening is a good place to start. As planetary heart intelligence matures, all will understand that "equality" is a gateway to the next level of human efficiency and effectiveness.

15. Self-empowerment is about you and yourself—awakening the "take charge" within you. You may have tried self-management before, but go for it again—this time from the heart. It can work. Learn to be yourself and manifest your inner strength. By managing your ego nature from the heart, you can make a tough life good and a good life better. Being yourself allows your spirit to manifest and regenerates your life. What more would you want than to finally be your complete self?

16. Heart management is a way to connect with your inner spirit—a source of strength and intelligence which has no ceiling on its potential. Whatever belief system you adhere to, *the heart approach to stress management* can be a non-threatening, non-competing add-on. As you manage your energy expenditures, you become your own stress buster which is a high achievement for yourself and the planet. Sure it sounds too simple at times, but so did the YO-YO—it was simple, yet offered a profound gift to the planet in terms of the user-friendly fun it has provided. Follow your heart with sincerity and see for yourself—it's you who can make it work or not.

To Sum Up:

Caring more sincerely will help to regenerate all people systems. *It's a recipe for productive living that is yet to be taken seriously by most people.* If it seems like a long-range plan, then realize there are no short-range plans to bail out planetary stress. Care oils your system and prevents spark-knocks and friction. It's the most efficient cosmetic that you may ever invest in.

Humanity is only at the surface level of understanding the transformative energy of care and love. It's like lifting weights. If you practice loving more, then your heart power can develop to the level of producing self-empowerment. Everything else has been tried *but love,* so take advantage of the opportunity to dust off the ol' heart and love more. It adds refreshment to life, and youth to age. *Just Love People More* or *"Love Ye One Another" and see what results from this.* These are statements of energy economy, not religious platitudes or unapproachable idealisms. They are advanced mathematical equations for planetary transformation. The proof is in doing. The results of deeper love and care will find you more quickly if you don't constantly look over your shoulder to see if the flower you planted is growing. You can change the world by managing yourself and building your capacity to Love.

In Closing

The basic message here is that stress is on the increase but you have a built-in system of stress relief—Self Empowerment. This can be achieved by learning to follow your heart with sincerity. People can try all kinds of exercise programs to get fit but the one that usually works is the one they practice *sincerely*. Being sincere in your efforts brings the truly effective results. Notice the deeper response and facilitation that you give to people when they approach you with sincerity—as in a sincere apology or request. If it works on you, it will work for you.

No book or system is going to give a quick fix for stress that doesn't require an exercise of effort. People know this inside, yet they still search for that one book or tape which will instantly make everything all right. The power to make things all right can be found within the heart of each person and this book is an effort to facilitate that realization. You already experience heart feelings and head thoughts throughout the day. It's just a matter of identifying them and bringing them into harmony and cooperation with each other. People experience head/heart balance naturally at times, but with practice you can do it consistently.

If you are not in agreement with some of the philosophical ramblings in the book, realize they are just opinions and leave them be. But underline and re-read the make-sense that feels right to you. This will help you remember to shift your energy to your heart when you're experiencing extra tension on the job, in a relationship, or in any situation where *remembering* could save you energy. Use the book for review. You already know much about the heart approach to life. It's *remembering* to use the wisdom that makes it work for you.

I've said this a-plenty but let me squeeze it in just once more: Practice caring for and being more sincere with all people, especially yourself. A human being's nature is to love, but stress has caused people to retreat into mental shells to protect themselves from being vulnerable to life's distortions. This shuts the heart down and causes more stress. Loving is a more efficient and regenerative remedy for happiness than hiding from life. In a sleepy way, people know that but it is time for a wake-up call.

Remember that the *head* is one of your best assets. The *heart* has the wisdom and the capability to manage it. The joint venture between the two can sure make life flow much more smoothly. You have self-empowerment within you already and it's worth making a heart commitment to manifest it. Don't wait for stress release miracles to come from science or technology. You are the method, and following your heart unfolds the formula. Build your self-security from your source of strength within and make a strong commitment to being yourself. I genuinely hope the book has helped confirm to you what you already intuitively feel inside. Have fun unfolding life through the intelligence of your own heart. It's been warm. We'll talk again later.

Sincerely,

The Doc

❖ THE INSTITUTE OF HEARTMATH

The Institute of HeartMath is a non-profit educational and research organization founded by Doc Lew Childre. Drawing upon the diverse educational, professional and cultural backgrounds of the Institute's staff and associates — which include the fields of business, education, psychology, physics, math, communication, music, and art— the Institute has developed a system of energy-efficiency and self-empowerment called HeartMath™. The Institute's mission is to reduce stress in the world by helping people develop greater self-management, self-esteem, and self-empowerment, through a deeper understanding of "heart intelligence."

The Institute offers seminars based on the HeartMath system for businesses, schools, non-profit organizations, groups, individuals, and families. The seminars emphasize practical, simple tools to manage stress and enhance communication skills while increasing self-empowerment. Seminars are presented in a variety of formats, including on-site corporate productivity, school in-services, in-house staff development, as well as customized "learning vacations," including whitewater rafting, dude ranches, ski trips, and other fun experiences.

The SELF EMPOWERMENT seminar for businesses is designed to increase corporate care and productivity based on the techniques outlined in this book. The seminar features tools for increasing personal and organizational efficiency, enhancing communication and decision-making skills, cooperation and team-building, and Intui-Technology™.

The HEART SMARTS seminars are designed to help educators, parents, and human services professionals reduce stress and revitalize their caring impulse in their work with young people. They are based on the book, *Heart Smarts: Teenage Guide for the Puzzle of Life*, which has been approved as a textbook by the California Department of Education. THE BRILLIANT HEART: EMPOWERING THE GIFTED CHILD is a seminar designed for gifted and talented students, parents and educators, and is based on the HeartMath system.

The HEART EMPOWERMENT seminars are for individuals and non-profit organizations seeking creative ways to empower their personal mission while reducing stress. These seminars offer a dimensional perspective of heart/head intelligence and how to enhance the family feeling, especially during the next ten years.

For more information on seminars, contact:
THE INSTITUTE OF HEARTMATH
P.O. Box 1463 • Boulder Creek, CA 95006
408-338-6803 • 800-354-6284 • Fax 408-338-9861

ALSO BY DOC LEW CHILDRE

THE HOW-TO BOOK OF TEEN SELF-DISCOVERY:
Helping Teens Find Balance, Security and Esteem

Parents, educators, and teens alike will enjoy this new edition of Doc's popular first book, *Heart Smarts: Teenage Guide for the Puzzle of Life,* which was approved as a textbook by the State of California.

Here's what reviewers had to say about the first edition.

> "This is an unusual book and a very powerful one. It assumes that teenagers *can* develop self-esteem and self-control, and that they *want* to. Then it shows them how."
>> ***Religion Teacher's Journal***

> "Does an excellent job of introducing teenagers to their feelings—and to healthy self-esteem. I applaud Doc Childre for his sensitivity to the needs of young people and for this most excellent tool for teenagers, adults and teachers. I recommend it highly."
>> **Emmett E. Miller, M.D.**
>> **California Task Force to Promote Self-Esteem and**
>> **Personal and Social Responsiblity**

> "Teens learn self-management through *Heart Smarts*. This book shows practical ways teens can make true-to-themselves decisions in daily life, resulting in self-confidence and stress release."
>> ***The Adviser*, Future Homemakers of America, Inc.**

> " Helps teens learn how to deal with the resentments, judgments and boredom that keep them unfulfilled. Learning to care for others; to practice appreciation for people, places and things, and to not judge other people or themselves, are some of the "power tools" that Childre advocates to build the real security and self-esteem teenagers are looking for."
>> ***College Preview: A Guide for College & Career Bound Students***

$8.95 plus shipping and handling • Available September '92.

HEART ZONES:
A Musical Solution for Stress

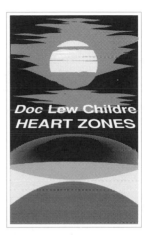

Music has the power to alter and change hormonal flows and has a serious vitamin-type effect on the mental and emotional aspects of our nature. "Music is like a food for the psyche. Unbalanced food leads to negative feedback in your system, whether it be physical food or food for the psyche (music, impressions, color, thoughts, etc.)," according to Doc Lew Childre, composer of *Heart Zones*. Both children and adults benefit from the right "vitamin-charged food".

"The Doc" designed *Heart Zones* to facilitate stress release and create an enhanced learning environment, while adding fun and balance to your mental and emotional well-being. The Doc adds, "*Heart Zones* is not intended to 'knock your socks off' on first impression. It is intended to give you a fun energetic atmosphere for putting your socks on in the morning or taking your socks off at night."

"I enjoyed **Heart Zones**. Very beneficial to patients to help them with stress management."

> **David J. Fletcher, M.D., Occupational and Preventive Medicine,**
> **Midwest Occupational Health Associates, Decatur, Illinois**

"**Heart Zones** is excellent for deep muscular relaxation. As a therapeutic tape, it is very different from all similar products I have used before. The compositions are inspirational and a refreshing change from the albums sold as 'New Age'. It's almost a whole new genre of music."

> **Marshall Gilula, M.D., Psychiatrist**

"I never thought I'd be saying this... but [Heart Zones] works. It really really works. When I need to relax, I put on cut 4. When I need to get going in the morning with a positive attitude, it's cut one. When it's time to write or get something done in a hurry, cut 3 brings focus and speed. The effects are discreet and effective and the instrumentation and presentation are right on the mark. [Heart Zones] is responsible for my high productivity!"

> **Scott Schuster, Editorial Director, Executive Programs, national magazine**

Cassette $9.95 • Compact disc $15.98 plus shipping and handling

The Hidden Power of the Heart:
How to Create a More Loving Environment for Yourself and Others
by Sara Paddison

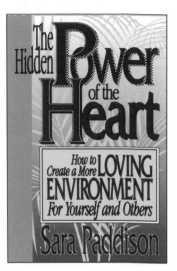

If you are searching for a new perspective on life, one of heart empowerment that brings fulfillment to every avenue of living, then read and practice the tools in this book! A new edition of the popular *Just Love the People*, this sensitive and profound book offers new insight on the hidden power of the heart. It reinforces how and why focusing on the heart will enrich our lives as well as the lives of everyone.

Here's what reviewers said about the first edition.

"Read this book; but even more important — follow its principle."
Deepak Chopra, M.D., author of *Quantum Healing*

"A powerful and rewarding collection of thoughts and tools that we all so dearly need to access our heart connection to Mother Earth."
Lynn Andrews, author of *Medicine Woman, Jaguar Woman*

"... a lovely book on the cure of 'people problems'."
Dr. Bernard Jensen, Bernard Jensen International

"A simple, straight-forward message of how to be happy in an increasingly complex and frightening world. Both thought-provoking and comforting."
Focus on Books

"This is the kind of book that you can sample when you feel the need. One passage on addictions helped me resolve some serious anger. You, too, will find useful passages."
Marie Friend, *Friend's Review*

$11.95 plus shipping and handling • Available Fall '92

ORDERING INFORMATION

To order books, tapes, and compact discs, please send check, money order or credit card information to:

Planetary Publications
P.O. Box 66 • 14700 West Park Ave.
Boulder Creek, California, 95006
408-338-2161/ 800-372-3100 • Fax 408-338-9861

- Please include shipping and handling costs: $2.50 for first item, $1.00 each additional item (book rate).
- For UPS delivery, add $1.00 to total shipping and handling. (Foreign residents should double the shipping and handling rates.)
- California residents include 7.25% sales tax.
- Visa, Mastercard, and American Express accepted. Please include expiration date, card number and full name on card.
- For convenience, place your order using our toll-free number—800-372-3100, 24 hours a day, 7 days a week, or by fax—408-338-9861.